JOSH PATRICK

AF208228

LIVING HOPE

CALLED OUT OF DARKNESS
AND INTO HIS LIGHT

HIM
PUBLICATIONS

Nashville, Tennessee

This sermon compilation by Josh Patrick serves as a profound source of inspiration. It underscores the importance of leaning on Jesus to infuse us with his enduring hope amidst life's challenges. Throughout his battle with cancer, Josh steadfastly upheld his faith in God, continuing to deliver Christ's teachings and share the good news far and wide. *Living Hope* stands as a testament, encouraging everyone that a bond with Christ paves the way to a life brimming with hope, regardless of the obstacles we face.

Dr. Darren Whitehead, founder and senior pastor,
Church of the City, Nashville, Tennessee

Josh Patrick's life and ministry epitomized hope. He talked to people individually about it, he preached corporately about it, and through his blog—and now adapted from sermons, this book—he wrote about it. Most importantly, Josh lived out God's teaching on hope every day . . . even to the very last days of his life. I loved serving with him on the staff at Harpeth Christian Church. I pray that the messages Josh has shared on hope from 1 Peter will change your life. This book is an inspiring and practical exposition that carefully follows the text of the first letter of the apostle Peter.

Bobby Harrington, lead pastor, Harpeth Christian Church,
Franklin, Tennessee; coauthor with Josh of
The Disciple Maker's Handbook

Living Hope is an inspiring and compelling look at how to walk out the Christian faith amid hardship. Josh Patrick shares that as humans and believers, pain will be part of our reality—and that spiritual maturity is being able to hold two things at once: joy and sorrow. Josh's wisdom on this topic was birthed through his real-life experiences, both as a pastor and as one who "fought the good fight" through a cancer journey. His honesty and wisdom allow us to be mentored by him. This is a handbook for how to face our trials and do so in a way that demonstrates our faith in real-time and ultimately creates a legacy of giving the glory to God in all things.

Amy Alexander, CEO and cofounder,
The Refuge Center for Counseling

Josh gave his entire life to the belief that God raising Jesus from the dead changed the entire course of human history. He lived, breathed, preached, and shared this good news. In Josh's book *Living Hope*, we get a glimpse into the heart of a man who wanted everyone to know the hope of Jesus. If the entire Christian faith hangs on this historical event—and I believe it does—we can spend our days celebrating the joy we have in God's defeat of death. Digest this book!

Josh Graves, author of *The Simple Secret*

Need hope? Look no further! Simple, instructive, and inspiring, this collection of adapted sermons from 1 Peter by Josh Patrick is a soul-nourishing feast of gospel hope. Full of wit and wisdom, *Living Hope* promises to lift the chin of every reader to behold again—or to behold for the first time—the never-failing hope of the gospel.

Nate Shurden, senior minister, Cornerstone Presbyterian Church Franklin, Tennessee

The letter of 1 Peter contains a message for our times! Josh Patrick offers us a gift in his exposition of it. His exposition is informative, practical, passionate, and moving. Based on the sure hope of resurrection, Josh calls us to embrace following Jesus by becoming Jesus in a world hostile to Jesus. This is a wonderful resource for churches, classes, small groups, and families, as well as one's own personal walk with God.

John Mark Hicks, retired professor of theology, Lipscomb University

While experiencing complex trials of his own, Josh Patrick eloquently testifies to the living hope of Christ aided by the perspective of the apostle Peter. This book is an engaging and inspiring read. Peter was not a man of great accomplishment but of great heart, making his perspective relatable and his lessons easily applicable. *Living Hope* epitomizes what it means to live with the hope of the risen Savior inside your heart.

Justin Moore, lead minister, Central Church of Christ, Athens, Alabama

Contents

To the most amazing Dad. Thank you for showing me what it looks like to embody living hope. When I think of you, I'm inspired to spread the gospel message wherever I go. My hope is that through your words in this book, we would change the trajectory of our lives toward heaven.

—Love, Lilly

To my Dad, who taught me to never give up even in the hardest season. Thank you for showing me that my only hope can be found in Jesus. I loved watching you live this out every day of your life.

—Love, Joy

To my Dad, who taught me to love always, persevere through the tough times, and to have hope through every moment.

—Love, Sarah

Foreword

In many ways, writing about my older brother, Josh Patrick, and Christian hope is basically the same. Some of my earliest memories consist of Josh preaching the gospel. Josh and I always shared a deep bond, and during his life, he stood as a faithful presence of hope to me. While we were ten years apart in age, the Lord called us both to be pastors, shepherds of God's flock. I'll always cherish sharing this sacred calling with my older brother.

One of my and Josh's mutual heroes, Eugene Peterson, once said that pastors are caught up in a "vocation of words"—not just any words but holy, living, and active words. These are scriptural words, bearing witness to the Word made flesh, Jesus Christ. To know Josh as a preacher was to hear a steady and careful treatment of the biblical text met by homiletical passion and exuberance. There was a holy fire to Josh's life as a disciple and as a pastor.

Aspiring ministers, especially those engaging theological studies during seminary, are endlessly tempted to keep Jesus and the great doctrines of the faith up in the "ivory tower," safe and separate from the messiness of living rooms, kitchens, and classrooms. But Josh had no time for a merely abstract Christian faith.

Knowing God, for Josh, was to *see* the great truths of Scripture—like faith, hope, love, grace, and fear of the Lord—take on flesh in his actual life. Josh loved hearing the Word, studying the Word, and preaching the Word; but Josh's supreme commitment and gift was *practicing* the Word, which made his preaching all the more compelling.

> Here's where hope comes in.

Hope was not a theological concept or a sentimental holiday card; hope for Josh was specifically *resurrection hope*. Inspired by one of Josh's greatest influences, N. T. Wright, the resurrection was home base for Josh. When he proclaimed the good news of Jesus, regardless of the text or subject at hand, you heard resurrection hope. *Christ is alive!* We all felt this truth at his preaching.

With confidence I can say that the primary commitment of Josh's life was to announce the hope of Jesus everywhere he went, no matter where he was or who he was with. Whether he was behind a pulpit or enduring chemotherapy treatments, resurrection hope was his anchor—not just his homiletical anchor in the pulpit but also an anchor for his soul.

You will notice discussion questions at the end of the book for your use. I am honored to have written these questions for your prayerful discussion among friends, family, and fellow members of your local church body. As you encounter these words, may you find a deep anchor for your soul in the risen and reigning Christ, who is our living hope. When all else fails, Christ remains steady, sure, and faithful—even to the end.

Rev. Matt Patrick
Advent, 2023

Preface

What is your legacy? What is it that you are leaving behind as you live out life here on earth? What is it that you want to be remembered for?

My late husband, Josh Patrick, is remembered for the hope he had in Christ. His greatest desire was to spread the hope of Christ to anyone who would listen. From the time he was a young child, he would stand in front of his parents in their living room with a Bible in his hand and deliver a sermon. Josh earned scholarships for speeches he presented in high school. He had an internship at a local church in Huntsville, Alabama, during high school, learning all he could about ministry work. In college, he began preaching every opportunity he had in order to share the words of Christ with others. He went on to graduate school and continued to preach full time for over thirteen years.

As I sorted through the collection of sermons that Josh left behind when he went to live eternally in heaven, I knew that I had to continue sharing them with the world. Josh started a sermon series on 1 Peter on Easter Sunday in 2018. This book is the treasury of that series, focusing on the importance of hope through the lens of following Christ. The ten chapters of this book were adapted from the sermons Josh preached at Harpeth Christian Church from that April through July.

Peter is called the "apostle of hope," and his primary message is to trust the Lord, live obediently no matter your circumstances, and keep your hope fixed on God's ultimate promise of deliverance. Josh's sermons highlight these topics and remind us all that no matter what trial or situation we are suffering through at the present moment, we can hold on to the promise that our eternal inheritance is on the horizon, as we hope in the return of Jesus Christ and the eternal glory we will share with him.

Josh's brother, Matt Patrick, who wrote the Foreword, is currently a pastor in Huntsville, Alabama, and he continues Josh's legacy of blessing and encouraging people daily to grasp the hope that is found in God's Word. One of Josh's roles in ministry was meeting with small group leaders and creating content for weekly study times. Josh would craft questions each week based on his sermons for small groups to use. I wanted Matt to provide a tool for you as the reader to continue to use Josh's sermons to engage with others and have questions ready for discussion of each sermon. Matt has created discussion questions for each chapter so you can use this book as a tool to study with others, in a group or in a one-on-one setting.

My prayer is that as you read these sermons from 1 Peter, you will be encouraged to walk daily in the joy of the living hope that is found from the promises of God.

— Joni Patrick

The Mythical Hope

A Sermon on 1 Peter 1:3–9

Praise be to the God and Father of our Lord Jesus Christ! In his great mercy he has given us new birth into a living hope through the resurrection of Jesus Christ from the dead, and into an inheritance that can never perish, spoil or fade. This inheritance is kept in heaven for you, who through faith are shielded by God's power until the coming of the salvation that is ready to be revealed in the last time. In all this you greatly rejoice, though now for a little while you may have had to suffer grief in all kinds of trials. These have come so that the proven genuineness of your faith—of greater worth than gold, which perishes even though refined by fire—may result in praise, glory and honor when Jesus Christ is revealed. Though you have not seen him, you love him; and even though you do not see him now, you believe in him and are filled with an inexpressible and glorious joy, for you are receiving the end result of your faith, the salvation of your souls.

— 1 Peter 1:3–9

A recent nationwide poll posed a simple yet intriguing question: What one phrase do most people want to hear and have spoken to them? Likely, you can guess the most common response. People want to hear one thing more than anything else, a simple trio of words: *I love you.* The second most commonly given response was a bit of a surprise—for me, that is: *You are forgiven.* And the third most common response I would not have guessed (but maybe it does make sense after all): *Supper is ready.*

Those three statements offer the promise of hope in one way or another—hope for being known and valued, hope for being forgiven, and hope for being well-fed. We all hope, plain and simple. But our culture is deeply confused about what real hope is and how to have it. It would seem the world finds it cool to be riddled with doubt and cynicism. Consider, though, where all that doubt and cynicism has brought us.

When Jesus' dead heart started beating again, God unleashed a revolution of hope that continues even now to redeem, restore, and resurrect lives all over the world. Jesus, the child of a common carpenter and a teenage girl from a no-name town—who never wrote a book or ran for office, a man with a rag-tag bunch of unimpressive rejects for friends—turned the world on its end by stepping out of the darkness of his own grave unhindered, unharmed, and untouched. He walked out into the aching, desperate, hopeful world completely, fully alive.

> God unleashed a revolution of hope.

Hope appears in many ways. We know it as longing, yes, but it's also there in every campaign promise and film storyline. Hope is woven into countless songs, books, conversations, and dreams. We are simply a people who hope. It's a deep and primal part of our being. The crucial difference we need to understand for our own lives is between having a dead hope and having the living hope which comes from God alone. I aim to make that distinction clearer by looking closely at a passage from 1 Peter.

In 1 Peter 1:3–9, Peter explores all it means to have godly hope in the midst of challenging times. Living hope is hard to find if you're distracted and deluded by false, dead hope. Myths about hope are everywhere, stubbornly embedded into our culture. We likely don't even know they're there, but they are and they're hurting us. These myths deceive and destroy people. I want to expose and correct five of the prevailing myths about hope using this passage from 1 Peter as a guide.

Myth 1: Hope Comes from People, Places, and Things

Things we can see. Things we can touch. That's what we turn to, but why? Why do we put our hope in people, politicians, presidents, pastors, places, and empty promises? Some parents hope in their children and attempt to vicariously experience the promises of hope through them. Some put their hope in places. Some try to return to the past, wanting to recreate a romanticized version of their former life, thinking that if only that season could be relived then hope would return.

We love our things: Money. Work. Health. We obsess over our appearance, our reputation, and our platform. People even put hope in religion itself, in its rituals and traditions. I think in our better moments we know that none of these things can produce real or lasting hope. Merely slowing down and taking a step back reveals that truth. Living, lasting hope cannot come from such things. Believing and acting as if it can will lead to dead ends. Other people, places, or things being a source of hope is only a cleverly devised myth.

The truth about hope is that it comes from God alone.

Look with me at verse three:

> In his great mercy he has given us new birth into a living
> hope through the resurrection of Jesus Christ from the dead.
> (1 Pet. 1:3)

God is merciful. Peter—eyewitness and close friend of Jesus—says that God in his great mercy gives us good things, and when we put our confidence in the risen Christ, he causes us to be born again.

In Romans 15, God is given a special title, one no other rival god has ever shared: "God of hope." Here's what that means for us: When you connect with God, you open yourself up to hope. When you detach from God, you walk away from hope. When you put your confidence in Jesus, you are empowered with the same power that breathed life back into his lifeless body. With hope, you can persevere through tremendous adversity. With hope, you can smile in the face of pain and believe the best is yet to come. Hope comes from God alone. And in his great mercy, he wants every single one of us to have it.

Myth 2: Hope Fades Over Time

What do you think about your physical health? Do you feel hopeful about what you see in the mirror? I know people who look in the mirror searching for wrinkles and lines, feeling disturbed at the sight of them because culture has preached loudly that aging can be stopped, that we aren't as mortal as we fear. Well, the hard realities of life can trick us into letting go of hope. The longer we live, the harder it is to keep hope around, right? Consider all the lies running rampant about marriage. That initial spark of love? The butterflies? It will gradually fade. Just give it enough time. Whether it ends in divorce or death, it will only become worse and worse as time moves along. Why keep hoping when faced with such a dim reality?

They say hope is unsustainable. Once you lose it, you're not getting it back. Enjoy it while you have it because it's going to be a fleeting thing. It's gone with your health, with your marriage, with life. But that's all a myth. The truth about genuine hope is that it grows over time. The hope that comes from God is alive.

Think about it from a linguistic perspective. What does it mean for something to be

Hope grows over time.

alive? That thing must grow, expand, deepen, or reproduce. In his great mercy, God has given us new birth into a living hope, as verse three says, "through the resurrection of Jesus Christ from the dead." When you meet an older saint who's been trusting and following Jesus for decades, whose life has been anything but perfect and easy, yet there's still a sparkle in their eye, you're seeing living hope. Someone has living hope if they seem to have a not-quite-explainable *something* in their life and in their spirit, if somehow by the grace of God they are hopeful in the midst of life. It's as though this person lives with one foot in heaven while still on the earth.

Paul says in 2 Corinthians that we never give up: "Though outwardly we are wasting away, yet inwardly we are being renewed day by day" (4:16). While aging brings decay, something within us is growing all the while, getting sweeter and sweeter, for our present troubles are small. Our present woes won't last very long, yet they will produce for us a glory vastly outweighing them, a glory that will last forever. We don't look to the troubles we can see now, but rather we fix our eyes on things that cannot be seen; for the things we see now will soon be gone, but the things we cannot see will last forever. There's more going on than what we can see.

Yes, sometimes it gets hard. Yes, we age. Yes, we live in a fallen, twisted, sin-ridden, evil-dominated world. But the clock is ticking, and with every passing second, the return of Jesus comes still closer.

Myth 3: Hope Is an Unrealistic Dream

I went to a reputable online dictionary a couple of days ago looking for synonyms and antonyms of hope. I'm kind of a word junkie. I was shocked to find the words "fact," "reality," and "truth" listed as antonyms of hope. These words are representing the opposite side of hope.[1] How misleading!

There's a false narrative out there about hope, saying that if you understand real life then you will assume the worst because that's what smart people do. We may have seemingly solid reasons to believe the world is broken. Relationships deteriorate. Dreams dissolve. We are burned and broken by circumstances and people. Loved ones get sick.

We suffer losses in this life, but that's due to living in a dark and decaying world. So if that's all we're willing to see, then hope is only a distant dream, no more than a fairy tale. God wants more for us, though. All this world can give is dying hope.

> God offers living hope.

The truth of the matter is that hope, authentic hope, is rooted in the past. In some general sense, the hope of God is anchored to a specific moment in history. Again, in verse three, "In his great mercy he has given us new birth into a living hope through the resurrection of Jesus Christ from the dead."

Christ's resurrection is the epicenter. It is the wellspring of hope. When you see the world through the lens of the empty tomb, it's hard not to become a hope addict. It's not that you won't let it go; it's that it won't let go of you because it colors and influences every nook and cranny of your life. Those who follow Jesus are therefore prisoners of hope.

There are truths and realities that can only be apprehended and taken in if we're willing to move beyond what can be experienced with our five senses. Peter, the author of the words we're focusing on right now, is a perfect case study of this. He was an eyewitness, recruited by Jesus to follow him. Jesus would eventually call Peter to preach. When the two first met, Peter was a very different person, a nobody. He was actually a questionable man—not much education, young, no wisdom, extremely impulsive. Have you ever been around a person who speaks whatever comes to their mind the moment that it enters their thoughts? Such a person is likely hard to be near. There's Peter for you.

Yet Jesus felt drawn to him. Jesus called out the good in him. He gave Peter a miraculous makeover of the heart. The Peter we see in the New Testament once Jesus had begun his transformation is a very different kind of man. Peter speaks about how he saw Jesus after he rose from the dead. He was with him, touched him, and ate breakfast with the risen Christ. He spoke not in metaphor, not of hallucination. What he spoke of was real, so much so that Peter gave his whole life to it—and eventually, like many others, for it.

Here's the moment of truth. A few years ago, it dawned on me that the quality and trajectory of my life would be determined by how I answered a single question: *Is Jesus dead or is he alive?* He cannot be both. We have to pick one, and our life will reflect that choice. Up to this point in your life, how have you lived?

If he's dead, he's a fake. He's a liar, a fraud. If he's dead, the story isn't true, and we're wasting our time—he wouldn't be a leader worth following. If he's dead, then that would make Christianity the most destructive and elaborate hoax in history. If he's dead, then faith is totally pointless. If Jesus was not raised from the dead, then every one of us remains dead in sin, still responsible for paying the price of our sins. If he's dead, then every church in the world should forever close their doors. If Jesus is dead, we are a bunch of pitiful, misguided fools, basing our lives on a lie. If he's dead, any notion of hope beyond the grave is worthless.

However, if he's alive—if Peter and all the eyewitnesses in the New Testament who risked their lives to get this story on the street are telling the truth, if all the people who say "The same Jesus who walked out of the grave has walked into my life and is changing me and giving me hope" are not a bunch of liars and lunatics, and Jesus really is alive—then everything Jesus said about God, the human condition, and the world is true.

It means he's not just a good man. You can't just call him a good teacher or a nice guy. If he's alive, you can't just put him on the buffet line of world religions and think he's one option among many. If he's alive then he is in a class all his own, towering above the rest. He alone has the power to bring dead things to life. If he's alive, his movement is unstoppable, and his people should have no fear.

If Jesus is alive, then he demands and deserves our absolute allegiance. If he's alive, we should stop what we're doing and fall to our knees to acknowledge his unsurpassed brilliance, unrivaled power, and unchallenged authority, then rearrange our entire lives here, now, pronto. Our first priority is his lordship. If he's alive, then his resurrection is the game changer for all of time and history. The day of his resurrection, my friends, is the greatest day to have ever gone by on the calendar. Hope is not a faint dream; it is rooted in reality. Jesus overcame death.

Myth 4: Hope Is a Virtue

Hope being a virtue makes sense at first. At the end of 1 Corinthians 13, Paul lists faith, hope, and love as three important, transcendent things in life. So it's tempting to interpret him to mean, "Go do your best at showing love, having faith, and sharing hope." But how many of us have ever loved someone? We sometimes think that, with effort alone, we'll just figure it out and go love better. What about faith?

Can you really believe something by simply telling yourself to believe it? It's a great recipe for losing faith at some point.

The same goes for hope. You can't force hope any more than you can force love or faith. You cannot muster it up out of sheer will. Hope in its purest form is not a human virtue. True, the last thing the world needs is another critic or cynic. We need encouragers and life-givers. Cynicism doesn't solve problems; it only complicates the problems we already have. A marriage doesn't turn around because both parties decide to wallow in despair. No one breaks free from an addiction by being hypercritical of everyone else. No one finds the good life by refusing to hope.

God graciously offers the truth that hope is not a virtue. Hope is a power. It's a power when we trust and follow the risen Jesus. The Holy Spirit catalyzes a supernatural process of redemption and transformation that cannot be experienced in any other way apart from Jesus. Disciples of Jesus are filled and fueled by hope—uncommonly resilient and joyful through all of life's experiences.

Here again is what Peter wrote, to paraphrase: *God's power protects you through your faith until salvation is revealed at the last time. This makes you very happy, even though now for a short time, different kinds of troubles may make you sad. These troubles come to prove that your faith is pure, and this purity of faith is worth more than gold, which cannot be proved to be pure by fire but will ruin. But the purity of your faith will bring you praise and glory and honor. When Jesus is revealed to you, you have not seen Jesus, but you love him. You cannot see him now, but you believe in him. So you're filled with a joy that cannot be explained, a joy full of glory* (1 Pet. 1:5–8).

That's the power of living hope. It carries you and gives you access to other treasures like joy and peace. I've thought a lot about this text in the last few years, and what a great anchor it's been for me and my family. I've thought about my friends, those who've gone through struggles and hit the worst kind of hard times. They came to the end of their own resources, and then God found them there and gave them hope. Now they have their own stories of hope to tell. There are stories of hope all throughout our churches. Praise God. I want to share with you one of these stories.

Aaron grew up in a Christian family with Christian parents. He met his wife, Marissa, and a few years after that, they were married. Everything was good; everything was great—and then life happened. Their first daughter, Natasha, was with them for four days before passing away.

Aaron stuffed things down deep inside and compartmentalized in order to keep going. Fast forward a few years, and finally he reached a boiling point. He had learned several coping mechanisms for dealing with stress and life's disappointments. These were anything from overeating, to looking at pornography, to drinking too much alcohol.

He was completely hopeless. He now faced potentially losing his wife and children and family—what he had worked so hard to have for so long. He felt the weight of the world on his shoulders, as if it were his job to keep people happy and not disappoint them. He knew he had to start over.

One evening when they were apart from each other, Marissa texted Aaron, saying, "I'm willing to fight for our marriage." From that point, they both decided to fight alongside one another. After attending Celebrate Recovery a couple of times, Aaron heard in the back of his head a voice saying, "You have never fully trusted me before. Just let go." He saw at last what he needed to do: trust God and let go. He needed to stop trying to live life under his own power all the time, because every time he tried to do so, he failed.

> "I'm willing to fight for our marriage."

In the past, Aaron had relied on biblical trivia facts as having a relationship with Christ. In the past few years, he's begun to have a personal, intimate relationship with Christ. Aaron had lost all hope for his marriage and for his life, but he made a choice to trust God and hope in his promises. Hope was not a virtue Aaron came to possess on his own. It was a gift to him from God.

Myth 5: Hope Is Fragile

The fifth and final myth concerns the fragility of hope. We can act as if hope is here one minute and gone the next, depending on what's happening in life, but authentic hope from Jesus is indestructible. We're born again into a living hope through the resurrection and "into an inheritance that can never perish, spoil, or fade" (1 Pet. 1:3–4). We have been given a hope that cannot be taken away, and we can then act out of that unremovable hope.

Nothing motivates passion and effort like hope. Hebrews 6:18 says that we who have run for our very lives to God have every reason to grab the promised hope with both hands and never let go. This hope is an unbreakable spiritual lifeline, reaching past all appearances to the very presence of God. Paul writes in Romans:

> Nothing can ever separate us from God's love. Neither death nor life, neither angels nor demons, neither our fears for today nor our worries about tomorrow—not even the powers of hell can separate us from the God's love. No power in the sky above or in the earth below—indeed, nothing in all creation will ever be able to separate us from the love of God that is revealed in Christ Jesus our Lord. (Rom. 8:38–39, NLT)

I don't know who you are. I don't know what you're walking through. I don't know the baggage you're carrying around. I don't know the things keeping you up at night. But I do know this: wherever you are—wherever that may be—there is a lifeline directly from heaven before you.

I encourage you to reach out and grab the lifeline of hope with both hands. Consider the body and the blood of Jesus. Consider what the death and resurrection of Jesus has already accomplished for you.

Listen to these promises. We know that God raised the Lord Jesus from the dead. He will also raise us up. God loves us deeply. He is full of mercy. He gave us new life because of what Jesus has done. He gave us life even when we were dead in sin. God's grace has saved you. God has "rescued us from the kingdom of darkness and transferred us into the Kingdom of his dear Son, who purchased our freedom and forgave our sins" (Col. 1:13–14, NLT).

I find that a lot of church people live in a pressure cooker of sorts—call it "spiritual performance anxiety." They live for the victory. They know about the inheritance. They know about the hope. They know about heaven, and the new heaven and new earth, and the ultimate victory of Jesus. But then they live as if they have to earn it. So they live constantly checking themselves, constantly worried and concerned—unable to lean into the joy of a living hope in the promises of God.

There are others who don't live *for* the victory. They live *from* the victory. They know it's there. They believe the promises—like the one from Peter, for example. And yes, they exert great effort and offer great sacrifices, but they don't do it so they can attain to or hold on to something. They do it because they believe Jesus when he said, *You already have this, it's waiting for you.*

◆

Father, we give you praise and honor and glory for raising your son Jesus from the dead. Help us have faith that this is not just a mere story in an old book but my ultimate reality. We pray you would help us in the midst of every fear, worry, doubt, and cynicism, that you would guide us out of every moment of confusion, apathy, and discouragement, and that you would empower us to dispel the myths about hope our culture preaches and help us to run hard after you, the God of living hope. In Jesus' name, amen.

A Claim, a Command, and a Craving

A Sermon on 1 Peter 1:22–2:3

> *Now that you have purified yourselves by obeying the truth so that you have sincere love for each other, love one another deeply, from the heart. For you have been born again, not of perishable seed, but of imperishable, through the living and enduring word of God. For, "All people are like grass, and all their glory is like the flowers of the field; the grass withers and the flowers fall, but the word of the Lord endures forever." And this is the word that was preached to you. Therefore, rid yourselves of all malice and all deceit, hypocrisy, envy, and slander of every kind. Like newborn babies, crave pure spiritual milk, so that by it you may grow up in your salvation, now that you have tasted that the Lord is good.*
>
> *— 1 Pet. 1:22–2:3*

Peter is quite possibly the most qualified human on earth—other than Jesus, who was God and human—to write about the unbelievable inheritance of hope that can never perish, spoil, or fade. If you know anything about Peter's story, then you know that he was just like us. He made the same mistakes we do. He would often act before thinking things through. He was a "ready, fire, aim" kind of person. He had a lot of passion. He was a blue-collar, no-name fisherman with no dreams to speak of about his future. He looked like an average kind of person, one you would ignore and move past while walking down the street.

Jesus found him on the fishing dock and called him to a life of discipleship. Jesus worked through him. He broke him, and he put him back together again. Peter denied Jesus three times when Jesus needed him most. Instead of chastising or condemning Peter, Jesus forgave him, showing grace upon grace. Then at the last, Jesus said, *I have something for you to do. Feed my sheep.* It was near the end of Peter's life that the apostle wrote the letter we have now.

We have a piece of personal correspondence from Peter, an eyewitness and friend of Jesus, someone who knew Jesus better than most. To think that we can read his words and hold his letter in our hands! It's a stunning, amazing, and remarkable gift. Peter would go on to be one of the most compelling articulators of the gospel. In 1 Peter 1:22–2:3, he invites us to take Jesus seriously again with a claim to believe, a command to obey, and a craving to follow.

A Claim to Believe

Let's begin with the claim in verse twenty-three: "You have been born again." This is a central point of Christian belief, not a throwaway phrase. It's not something to gloss over or rush past.

You have been born again.

It's the easiest part of the passage to move on from because we all know it already. Of course, we've been born again. Could we just marvel at that together? *You have been born again.* You have been reborn. You have been repurposed. You have been brought from death to life—renewed, redeemed, resurrected. As Paul would say, you've been transferred from a kingdom of darkness and brought into a kingdom of light. Your sins are forgiven. You're a new kind of person. Something miraculous and otherworldly and mysterious has happened to you. Spiritual renewal is the miraculous working of God to bring us out of death and into life.

> You have been brought from death to life—renewed, redeemed, resurrected.

The New Testament constantly reminds believers of this reality. Why do the writers keep repeating themselves?

You've been born again, remember?

Jesus has brought you from death to life.

The resurrected life of Jesus is in your soul.

You are walking in newness of life.

Your old ways are gone.

This old-life-new-life theology is so prominent in every section of the New Testament, yet somehow it's easy to miss the weight of it. It's easy to move past it and think it's for new believers or pre-believers or whatever we call people who are not yet following Jesus. It's for those people, not for those of us who have crossed over into active belief already. But it is for everyone who calls themselves a Christian and a follower of Jesus—for this is the fruit borne out of our living hope.

The New Testament was written by disciples for disciples. Peter's letter was not an evangelistic, "get the gospel on the street" letter. It was a "remind these people who they are" letter. Tell them the truth. Go back to the basics because we will never outgrow our need to hear it again. We have been born again. So many forces pull us away from that truth. We return to the remnants of our old life, or sometimes they roar back into our lives and threaten our faith, blinding us from seeing the goodness of God again. We need to be reminded of the living hope that only comes from Christ Jesus.

I heard a story about a forty-year-old mom of three from Minnesota named Jennifer Jones.[2] She was misdiagnosed for most of her life with asthma and allergies, essentially chronic breathing trouble with all kinds of physical limitations and struggles. One day, she went to a new doctor who told her the other healthcare professionals that had been observing her had been wrong. He told her she had cystic fibrosis—a degenerative and fatal respiratory condition. The fact that she had lived with it for so long baffled the doctor, and he recommended a double lung transplant. He told her she needed new lungs or she would die. So she got on the list, and she waited. She ended up getting the lung transplant. Just before the surgery, she was on oxygen twenty-four hours a day, and her lungs were reduced to 10 percent capacity.

Imagine how Jennifer Jones must have felt when taking her first breath after the lung transplant. I imagine she felt as though she had been brought out of death, like she was returning to life. Now think about your own conversion. When Jesus breathed his life into us, it may not have felt so dramatic. But have you ever witnessed a baptism where someone comes out of the water and it looks like a fan is blowing on their face at 400 miles per hour—where they can't stop smiling and their joy is contagious? What is that about? Have you ever seen somebody repent and experience the grace of forgiveness, or know someone whose marriage or broken relationship has been restored? Do you remember how happy and full of hope they were?

You have been born again.

If you trust and follow Jesus, you can say with rock-solid confidence, "I've been born again." It's a past event with continuing effects. Jesus has accomplished everything necessary. He offers forgiveness, hope, and peace. When we pledge our lives to him, he removes our shame, our guilt, and our condemnation. He gives us new birth instead—a gift of grace.

> *It's not about works. It's not about earning.*
> *It's about receiving in faith.*

After the new birth, we have a part to play. God didn't cause us to be born again into a living hope to disable us and demotivate us. Nothing motivates obedience and passion like God's grace does. A life filled with hope does not remain stagnant but grows deeper, fuller, and more alive. The living hope Christ gives invites our participation in the process of sanctification. He includes us because he loves us and wants to be with us. We were redeemed once, and it counts for always, but our sanctification relies on listening to God's callings and following in his steps.

I heard a story about a pastor who was about to go into heart surgery. He asked the cardiologist, "Can you fix my heart?"

The doctor told him yes. After the twelve-hour surgery, right before he was discharged from the hospital, his wife asked the doctor, "What about my husband's future quality of life? What will that look like?"

The doctor paused and then said, "I fixed his heart, but the quality of his life is up to him."

Look at your own story and consider how God has been shaping you. What forces have been shaping and influencing you throughout your life? Look at the people who you think of as spiritually mature. What do you notice? They're close to God, and they walk closely with God. You will find that God grows people with two main strategies: spiritual disciplines and suffering. Now, how they look and how they get expressed is different, but you are likely to find those two threads running through everyone's story.

After our new birth God puts us on a track to grow and become more like Jesus. That is his agenda for us. He desires us to have the heart and mind of his son. He longs for all his children to love like Jesus. His first strategy for shaping us into a Christlike person is opening doorways for his Spirit to come in through the disciplines: prayer, Scripture, fasting, confession, and community. Those are things we either choose to do or neglect to do, and we neglect them at our own cost—forfeiting grace.

His other strategy challenges us more deeply, and it's not so much about what we do. It's about what happens to us—the trials, struggles, and unpredictable stressors that happen in our lives. When we are faced with those things, God is not destroying us but drawing us to a deeper place in Him, to know him in a fuller and more meaningful way.

The text says we've been reborn, but not just to enjoy life. Of course, we do enjoy it, but we've been reborn for *love*, which is a command to obey.

A Command to Obey

The command is straightforward. In verse twenty-two, Peter tells us to love one another deeply from the heart. Nothing will make you weary like trying to love someone who gives a shallow love in return. Shallow, insincere love is easily irritated and inconvenienced.

Such a love comes from a selfish place. Insincere love uses people for improvement in life or status and only wants to love when being offered something in return. I'm sure you know how hard it is to be in a friendship or a relationship like that.

Jesus' kind of love is deep—pouring out of our hearts, the deepest part of us. You can see his kind of love easily. You know it when you experience it, and you probably know what it feels like to be prompted to demonstrate it. You think to yourself, *Oh man, this is going to require more than I have. So I'm going to have to tap into a power greater than myself to do this.*

His kind of love offers hope, grace, and mercy. It sees the good in others and calls it out. His is the kind of love that takes action more than being merely words alone. And it's not based on emotion but on the fact that we have been scandalously, ridiculously, extravagantly loved by God. Now, when that love gets ahold of you, you share it with others.

Five Enemies of Love

Several years ago, Oscar-winning actor Jeff Bridges gave a personal interview and was asked to identify his worst character defect. He said:

> We have been scandalously, ridiculously, extravagantly loved by God.

> Not loving enough. . . . Not having enough compassion, empathy, wisdom. My wife and I have been married for thirty-six years. I'm deeply in love with her, but every once in a while we'll get into what I like to refer to as our "deep, ancient battle." It's always very elusive and it's hard to find the real kernel of it, but basically it is about this: "You don't get it. You don't get what it's like to be me." Neither of us really understands what it's like to be that other person.[3]

What Bridges is describing there is that love takes work. Loving well is an ancient battle, nothing new. It takes hard, purposeful work to imagine being in another person's skin and to understand the weight of the burdens they carry.

After recommending that we resolve to become people who love, Peter says that we should name and remove five enemies of love from our lives: "Rid yourselves of all malice and all deceit, hypocrisy, envy, and slander of every kind" (1 Pet. 2:1). This verse is an invitation to probe your own life and heart. Look at your relationships. Are one or more of these enemies lingering in your life?

Enemy 1: Malice

Malice is not a word thrown around too often. The term "malicious intent" stems from Psalm 139:20, when evil ones are speaking against and purposely insulting God. The term is also used in relation to legal issues. If, when you think of someone, the idea of harm or trouble befalling them doesn't hurt you or upset you, that's malice. If you want bad things to happen to a person because they've hurt you, then you're harboring malice. This enemy sneaks into our thoughts, often before we realize it, which is why it's so very important to guard our hearts (Prov. 4:23).

Enemy 2: Deceit

Nothing holds back love in a relationship quite like deceit. You know when you're being deceitful, I'm sure, but it can still be easy to fall into. Misleading someone or telling half-truths sometimes doesn't feel so wrong in the moment—maybe it even feels necessary. But our God calls us to speak and live out truth. There's no room for deceit in a love like Christ's. I'm grateful we have a God who will never ever deceive us.

Enemy 3: Hypocrisy

I don't know anyone who wants to be called a hypocrite. It's not a flattering term. Hypocrisy is doing one thing and saying another. It's expecting others to observe rules you're not willing to play by yourself. The core of hypocrisy is inauthenticity, projecting something different than who you really are. In the groundbreaking, data-driven book *unChristian*, David Kinnaman and Gabe Lyons present a survey of young millennials who are not part of a church.[4] They asked the individuals to offer feedback about Christians and the church. The young millennials spoke specifically on how they perceive Christians. The responses weren't surprising—but still a kick to the gut.

The overwhelming perception of Christians is that Christians are hypocrites, doing one thing and saying another.

Enemy 4: Envy

Envy is one of the seven deadly sins. It is what I would call a "respectable sin" in our day. There are big sins, ones we all avoid at all costs (or at least hide), and then there are respectable sins, ones we are comfortable with. Envy is a heart thing. You see someone, you want what they have, and you feel a sense of disdain because they have it and you don't. This often happens when we compare ourselves to others upon seeing someone else's perfect family, amazing vacation, new car, pristine house, and mess-free life. Then we feel inferior, and our hearts can get toxic fast. Envy is lethal when it comes to cultivating loving relationships.

Enemy 5: Slander

Slander has destroyed more church communities than any sin I've ever known. Slander happens when you're talking about somebody else. Maybe there's a kernel of truth in whatever you're saying, but you're only telling because you want to feel a little better about yourself and get some sense of satisfaction out of it. Slander shows up in all kinds of ways. It can even be cloaked in a prayer request. It's a close relation of gossip. I love Dave Ramsey's definition of gossip: when I bring you a problem you can't solve as it pertains to somebody else, that's gossip.[5] Well, slander is even worse, because it is a calculated attempt to speak not-so-good about somebody else. In the end, it's spreading falsehood even if a kernel of truth resides in your words. I long for God to create a church culture where we love each other well and do not have any slander.

These five things are not just character defects—they are relational diseases. They are maladies of the soul, enemies of love, terrible, no-good, nasty things. The text says, Peter says, and Jesus says: *rid your life of these things.* Get a plan, confess your struggles with these things, and wage war. Don't settle for living on autopilot, thinking, *I must be doing okay, so why worry*—because malice, deceit, hypocrisy, envy, and slander are far worse than they sound, and they cause serious harm in ways we may not see.

A Craving to Follow

Now let's turn to the craving Peter gives us to follow. In 1 Peter 2:2–3, he says, "Like newborn babies, crave pure spiritual milk, so that by it you may grow up in your salvation, now that you have tasted that the Lord is good."

I remember going to the Main Street Festival in downtown Franklin, Tennessee. There were food trucks, and I could smell everything. Walking down the street with my family, I spotted a hibachi food truck. Suddenly all I could smell was rice and chicken. Then there was a California food truck, and I smelled veggies and grilled chicken. There was lots of fried food as well. My nose was assaulted, my senses were stimulated, and I started feeling hungry. Before going to the festival, I wasn't hungry. Then I smelled all that food, and I couldn't even decide where to go.

Author Frederica Mathewes-Green addresses people who hunger for God's presence but rarely feel it. Writing to a church audience, this is what she says:

> My hunch is that you are already sensing something of God's presence, or you wouldn't care. . . . Picture yourself walking around a shopping mall, looking at the people and the window displays. Suddenly, you get a whiff of cinnamon. You weren't even hungry, but now you really crave a cinnamon roll. This craving isn't something you made up. There you were, minding your own business, when some drifting molecules of sugar, butter, and spice collided with a susceptible patch inside your nose. You had a real encounter with cinnamon—not a mental delusion, not an emotional projection, but the real thing. And

what was the effect? You want more, *now*. And if you hunger to know the presence of God, it's because, I believe, you have already begun to scent its compelling delight.[6]

Have you tasted and seen that the Lord is good? Have you had moments with God that were so satisfying and thrilling you wanted more?

When I read the second and third verses of 1 Peter 2—"Like newborn babies, crave pure spiritual milk, so that by it you may grow up into your salvation, now that you've tasted that the Lord is good"—I was confused. *Pure spiritual milk? Milk is for babies*, I thought. In another passage in Hebrews, it says for us to go beyond milk and get to the meat. So then, what are we going back to, infancy?

Peter essentially equates pure spiritual milk to organic food. It's pure and uncontaminated. It hasn't been processed; it's not mass-produced. Instead, it is good and soul-satisfying. He doesn't mean for us to *act* like babies. Think about a newborn baby. How do they *eat*? They eat often, they eat vigorously, and when they're hungry, everybody knows it.

Don't let your spiritual hungers fall asleep. Let them rise, let God fuel them—and eat. The world tells us to feed our flesh and starve our soul.

> I urge you not to let your soul famish.

Let us be people who crave pure spiritual milk and eat like a newborn would—often, vigorously, and unabashedly.

◆

Lord Jesus, help us to hear your voice. Help us to believe you are good and that your purposes for me are wonderful and redemptive. Help us not to be merely fascinated with ideas about you but

to encounter you intimately as the living and true God—who for-
gives sin, liberates from bondage, and heals wounds: the God who
answers our questions, and the God who gives us living hope. We
need you to guide us, Lord Jesus, and our families, in the decisions
we may have to make. In the trials we're walking through, Lord,
increase our faith. Give us peace, Jesus. You promised that your
sheep would hear your voice as the Good Shepherd. May it be so
now. In your name, Jesus, amen.

3

Remember Who You Are

A Sermon on 1 Peter 2:4–10

> *As you come to him, the living Stone—rejected by humans but chosen by God and precious to him—you also, like living stones, are being built into a spiritual house to be a holy priesthood, offering spiritual sacrifices acceptable to God through Jesus Christ. For in Scripture it says, "See, I lay a stone in Zion, a chosen and precious cornerstone, and the one who trusts in him will never be put to shame." Now to you who believe, this stone is precious. But to you who do not believe, "The stone the builders rejected has become the cornerstone," and, "A stone that causes people to stumble and a rock that makes them fall." They stumble because they disobey the message, which is also what they were destined for. But you are a chosen people, a royal priesthood, a holy nation, God's special possession, that you may declare the praises of him who called you out of darkness into his wonderful light. Once you were not a people, but now you are the people of God; once you had not received mercy, but now you have received mercy.*
>
> *— 1 Pet. 2:4–10*

This passage may be, in my humble and accurate opinion, the signature passage in the New Testament as it pertains to discovering who we are as the sons and daughters of God. A friend and trusted confidant once told me, "If you find yourself riddled with *What should I do?* questions, it's because you haven't got the *Who am I?* question settled." This one passage answers the questions *Who am I?* and *What am I here for?*

God's Gracious Posture

Peter could have said only one thing about us and our new identity in Christ, but he lists six things in the last two verses of that passage— six surreal, life-changing things. He piles them on one after another: You are a chosen people, a royal priesthood, a holy nation, God's special possession. You are not *a* people, but *the* people of God. Once upon a time you had not received mercy, but now you have.

It's strange language for sure. Imagine walking up to someone in the church lobby and saying, "Well, good morning, royal priest." That would be strange and awkward. That's the truth, though.

Here's another scenario I want you to imagine: You're walking down a busy street, and someone you've never met stops you to say, "Excuse me, you have the most beautiful eyes I have ever seen." You can tell they aren't angling for something. Their words aren't empty.

And they continue, "Wow, when the sun hits your eyes, it's stunning." Say they kept on, complimenting your hair, your skin, your smile, and then they just moved on, disappearing from your life forever. Well, you would likely blush. You might think, *That is the oddest thing to ever happen to me.* I'd also wager you'd never forget it. As the person walked away, you might be inclined to think that maybe they're not in their right mind. One kind word and you may forget it, but compliments heaped on top of one another are not easily erased from memory.

As I read 1 Peter 2:4–10, I felt as though it was too much. Peter's words are flattering at first, but he just keeps on going. He goes so far that my instinct is not to believe it. Peter is presenting a principle so crucial for us to see that, if we miss it, we will never understand how to read the Bible; we can never fully enter into a life of discipleship of trusting and following Jesus; and we can never fully understand who we are—much less who God is.

The principle is this: God's high calling for you and the hard things he commands you to do are preceded by God's gracious posture toward you.

The writer Austin Farrer once said, "[Christ] took us, and associated us with his divine life, even while we struggled against him."[7] And I'd say even when we don't realize we are struggling against him. God's posture toward us is one of mercy and forgiveness, and awareness of that reality is what causes us to obey freely, repent quickly, surrender fully, and express our faith boldly.

Peter asks us to do some very difficult things—suffer for the gospel, submit to authorities who are ungodly, and stand firm against tremendous hardship and opposition. But we can do those things because of God's already-shown grace, our living hope. God's high calling for you and the hard things he commands you to do are preceded by his gracious posture toward you.

Living Stones

Have you ever found yourself wanting someone else to change? This happens in parent-child relationships, marital relationships, and even friendships. Change isn't easy. Even more difficult to accept is the reality that we can't change other people. Before we look deeper into what Peter says about change and how we change, look at what he says concerning Jesus. Understanding who we are depends on first recognizing who Jesus is.

Peter says two things. First, that Jesus is treasured by some and rejected by others. Maybe you've noticed it before in your reading. Verse four says he was rejected by humans, then, "Now to you who believe, this stone is precious." If you're a believer—if you would self-identify as rescued, forgiven, and called by God in Christ—then Jesus is everything. But for those of us who are not there, who have gone the other way, who have chosen the route of self-rule and being our own God, then Jesus is repulsive. He threatens everything.

I ask myself sometimes—and perhaps you ask yourself this too— *Why am I so unchanged after all these years?* After all that God has done, after the many times I've prayed, "God help me," and he has, after all those people he has sent me to encourage me and teach me truth: *Why am I not more different?* After everything God has done, after all we've been through, why are we still not the people we know we should be? *Why are there so many broken places remaining in my life? Why is my faith so weak and my holiness so anemic and my zeal so shallow? Why do I seem so hopeless?*

I think it's partly because we're all afflicted with identity theft. We don't know who we are. We don't know who Jesus is at times, and we build our lives on stones that are anything but solid. Jesus is called a stone in that passage, meaning firm, secure, and unshakable. If Jesus is not the true foundation of our life, we might as well be walking on quicksand. If you feel like your life is a perpetual earthquake—one drama, one chaos, one storm after another—it may not be the circumstances you're in. It may be the foundation you're walking on.

> We're afflicted with identify theft, and we don't know who we are.

We can say the name of Jesus without embracing his call to take up our cross and follow him, without dying to ourselves. We can sing his praises without relying on his power. Scariest of all, we can identify with Christianity as a religion while still, if we're honest, worshiping the gods of our age: comfort, cash, success, and self-expression.

Living hope can't be faked.

It's quiet and gentle.

Dead hope, on the other hand, is loud and sneaks along any chance it gets. It's an excellent imposter, and we're too easily wooed into its embrace. You will realize you've let your living hope become temporarily trampled by the state of your heart, your spirit, and your behavior.

Look at your life honestly. How do you respond to difficulty? What do you treasure? Where do you place value? Are you treasuring Jesus or rejecting him? There is no middle ground with Jesus. He is either Lord of all or Lord of nothing. He either motivates allegiance and heartfelt praise or provokes ridicule and rejection.

The second thing Peter says about Jesus is that he is actively building his people—present tense, meaning ongoing action. In verse five, Jesus is *the* stone, and we are like living stones, being built into a spiritual house. Peter uses an architectural image to communicate something deep and perhaps mysterious, even a little surprising, about Jesus and his church. Let me repeat myself: It is *his* church. It is his church globally, and it is his church locally. Peter communicates here that the church is the house of God.

We are to be a dwelling where God lives—not a rectangular building with clean lines, but a shapeshifting, ever-morphing, supernatural, unpredictable, untamed, undomesticated, powerful organism that Jesus himself is building right here, right now. You are a part of it. We all are. And Jesus is going to use you. He is using you right now to build the church for his glory and for generations to come, just as he did with the original audience of Peter's words.

Early Christians in the Roman World

The world from which Peter wrote was a very religious place, with temples and priests and shrines everywhere. There were multiple spiritualities to choose from, lots of worldviews to consider, and lots of gods to worship. The earliest disciples of Jesus stood out distinctly in the Roman world. Christianity wasn't viewed as a tame, new religion, but rather as a dangerous development that foolishly challenged the status quo.

Did you know that the earliest Christians were often called atheists? At the martyrdom of Polycarp, a second-century bishop, the crowd shouted, "Away with the atheist!" Christians stood out as deeply irreverent, refusing to worship the gods of their age or go to the pagan priests or acknowledge the sanctity of the pagan temples. They refused to play along, which made them stick out, not only to the government but also to the rest of society.

Think about it: One month they're worshiping all the other gods, swimming with the other fish, going to the shrines, paying their respects, doing what's cool, and playing the game. Now they're embracing a strange message about a crucified man. Now their entire way of life has changed.

The world had never heard a message like Jesus' before. They were seen as foolish simpletons, not elite. One critic said, "These poor wretches have convinced themselves, first and foremost, that they are going to be immortal and live for all time."[8] This was odd and strange and objectionable, even for wise statesmen.

There was a tremendous social cost to trusting and following Jesus that in our day, and in our land, is hard to understand. Following Jesus in the first three centuries was not only demanding; it was dangerous. Roman Emperor Marcus Aurelius saw Christianity as a clear and present danger to be snuffed out at all costs. Many believers were fed to animals or burned alive. They were estranged and ostracized. They lost influence, power, money, and livelihood. Some lost everything.

The real question for us is this: Why aren't Christians today experiencing more persecution? Maybe because we have more in common with the gods of our culture than we can see.

Perhaps we suffer so little because we stand for so little.

Do you see now why Peter's words struck a chord with his original readers? You, God's special possession? Peter says this to those who feel the opposite: alienated, marginalized, and scorned. His words had to be immensely encouraging to those first Christians.

I want to consider what kind of predicament we are in right now as followers of Jesus in the current cultural climate. What does it mean to be faithful in honoring the Lord Jesus? What made those early Christians so dangerously different? What will make you and me so dangerously different?

Let us not only see God's nature as a forgiver of sin but also as a holy God who calls us not to play it safe and swim with the other fish in worshiping the gods of our day. Let's not only look at God, but at what this moment reveals about who we are and the predicament we're in. What does it say about us that the crucifixion of the eternal Son of God was required to set us free and forgive us? What does it say about us? What ugly, inconvenient truth does our culture not want us to see? It's the cross. It all goes back to the body and blood, to a crucified man giving up his life. It's through this we are given living hope.

Cascade of Compliments

Returning to Peter's cascade of six compliments, I'll go through three of them:

1. A Chosen People

Peter utilizes at least eight Old Testament references in this text. The original hearers would have immediately thought of God's choosing of Israel when Peter said, "You are a chosen people." But why did God choose Israel? God did not choose Israel because they were superior—morally, physically, or in any other way. Scholar Ed Clowney said, "God's people are chosen, not choice."[9] The Lord did not choose us because of how hard we work to be worthy.

Why are we God's prized possession? Because we have a gracious God. It is all because of his grace. Now, why is that so important, and what does it have to do with you here and now? In the circumstances you're walking through, it means you can give up trying to prove yourself. You can just stop. We did not choose God. He chose us. We did not find God. He found us. We did not rescue God. God rescued us.

Think about your life. Think about the earliest influences around you who spoke with the name of Jesus on their lips. I see my grandmother, my youth pastor, my coaches, my teachers, and my neighbors. I see my parents. I see people—beautiful, precious people—who came to me in their own brokenness, using their own stories and their own gifts to show me how good God really is.

You have your own cast of characters in your story, don't you? It's remarkable, really. If we don't see the grace of God tumbling toward us like tidal waves, we have every potential for falling headfirst into a crisis of faith. I've been in that place before. It's not good. It's not healthy. It's toxic and leaves you spiritually lifeless and hopeless.

Some of us, me included, will find ourselves living from the faulty belief that God only loves good people, that he will only love us if we clean up first, that he will only accept us if we're willing to become acceptable first. That is not the life-giving good news of grace that exists in the Bible. It is the soul-crushing message of every other world religion. Religion will tell you that God's acceptance only follows our own goodness before him. His truth is exactly the opposite. Grace comes first. The God that Jesus came to reveal shows his posture toward us in his grace.

God did not choose us for our worth, our ability to serve, our wisdom, or our moral purity. God chose us so that we may declare the praises of him who called us out of darkness into his wonderful light. That means we were not meant to declare our own praises or display our own worth. God's posture toward us is mercy and grace. We should use every nook and cranny of our lives to show people the truth that he feels the same way about them. Our friends, family, neighbors, and coworkers all need to see how good and beautiful God is.

2. A Royal Priesthood

Peter describes our new identity in Christ as a royal priesthood. That's another Old Testament reference from Exodus 19:6: "You will be for me a kingdom of priests and a holy nation." What does he mean? He means that the people of Jesus don't have priests anymore, and we also don't have temples or ritual sacrifices. *We* are the priests. *We* are the temples. Jesus was sacrificed for us. This is a shocking and revolutionary idea. Even today, priests are considered to have direct access to the Lord of the universe. This means there is a holy dignity in our lives.

Martin Luther was once approached by a man who asked him how he should be serving the Lord.[10] Luther said, "What are you doing right now? What's your job?" The man said, "I'm a shoemaker." Much to the man's surprise, Luther told him to make a good shoe and sell it at a fair price. He didn't say, "Go make Christian shoes." He didn't say, "Go, leave your business, and become a monk." He didn't tell him to legitimize his work by making it spiritual in some way. He didn't encourage him to ditch his job, but to change his perspective. He encouraged the cobbler to do whatever he set out to do with God-glorifying goals, motivations, and standards. To see yourself as a priest means to believe it's your job—not the pastor's job—to show and tell people how good Jesus is. We are all in this together as the church.

This is us. We are all ministers. We are all priests. We are called to be hospitable, to be forgiving and generous, to keep away from gossip. We are to become a people known for the quality of our lives and for how closely we walk with God. We are priests. We should be known for our holy and hope-filled lives and our God-glorifying words.

> We are all ministers. We are all priests.

3. The People of God

The final description will pull on your heartstrings. Look back at 1 Peter 2:10. Peter directly references the Old Testament book of Hosea: "Once you were not a people, but now you are the people of God; once you had not received mercy, but now you have received mercy" (1 Pet. 2:10; see also Hos. 2:23).

God came to a prophet named Hosea and told him to marry a woman named Gomer. God told Hosea then and there that she would be unfaithful. *But,* he told Hosea, *I want you to marry her so that you will have a better idea of how I'm feeling about my people right now* (paraphrased from Hos. 1:2).

So Hosea married Gomer, and she was a serial adulterer. She cheated on him and cheated on him and cheated on him. And God told Hosea that the part he'd been playing with Gomer was the part God had been playing with his people. God spoke about how his people were breaking his heart, bent on turning away from him.

Not too long after Hosea and Gomer got married, she had children. One child was named "not loved," and another one was named "not my people."

One day, Hosea was walking toward the city center, and he saw his wife on the auction block. She couldn't stop cheating. She'd had children with other men. She'd been abused in the worst possible way. She was degraded. She'd been sold into slavery.

God came to Hosea and said, "Buy her back. Return, and love that woman." So Hosea did. He bought her at a high price and took her home.

We don't know how the story ended. Like with many of the stories in the Bible, what we have is unfinished. We are invited to finish the story and head straight for Jesus. When the original readers heard, "Once you were not a people, but now you are a people of God; once you had not received mercy, but now you have received mercy," their hearts likely leapt out of their chests. They would have immediately understood the reference, how the part that Gomer played with Hosea was their place with God.

In Jesus, God bought us at a high price, not with gold but with his blood. Seeing that, our spirits and souls should be awakened and changed by the grace of God. Force of will hardens hearts, but the understood and accepted grace of God softens them. When you see God in Christ coming toward you, saying, "I know where you've been, and I know what you've done. Still here I am, and will be," you'll know there's nothing like it.

When God calls broken people into the light, they do not become perfect people—they become exposed people, which is both scary and glorious. God's glory doesn't shine the brightest through our perfections and our performances. It shines brightest through our brokenness and desperation. When we admit our neediness, when we broadcast our failings without fear, the light of God's grace shows precisely through our weaknesses.

Why are we so afraid to be real before him and before our fellow believers? Let me remind you: God's posture toward us is amazing, never-ending grace. Our best response can only be active, ongoing trust.

I want to ask you what parts of your life you are most reluctant to trust him with. Where is God calling you to change? What do you need to let go of? What does trusting Jesus look like in this season? Everything from this moment on in 1 Peter will be hard and challenging. He asks hard things of us—inconvenient, subversive, and difficult things. But before we get there, remember who you are:

> You are a chosen people, a royal priesthood, a holy nation, God's special possession, that you may declare the praises of him who called us out of darkness into his wonderful light. Once you were not a people, but now you are the people of God. Once you had not received mercy, but now you have received mercy. (1 Pet. 2:9–10)

◆

Lord, thank you for this word in 1 Peter. Thank you, Jesus, for finding us, restoring us, and forgiving us. Once we were not a people; now we are your people. Once we had not received mercy, but now we have it. I pray that you would remove anything in us that would keep us from seeing who we really are. I ask you, Lord Jesus, to take away anything in our lives that keeps us from seeing how good and beautiful you are. Would you give us a deep and profound awareness for your presence in our lives and remind us that your plans for us are good, Lord? Use us for your glory. I pray through Christ, our Lord, amen.

Become Who You Are

A Sermon on 1 Peter 2:11–17

> *Dear friends, I urge you, as foreigners and exiles, to abstain from sinful desires, which wage war against your soul. Live such good lives among the pagans that, though they accuse you of doing wrong, they may see your good deeds and glorify God on the day he visits us. Submit yourselves for the Lord's sake to every human authority: whether to the emperor, as the supreme authority, or to governors, who are sent by him to punish those who do wrong and to commend those who do right. For it is God's will that by doing good you should silence the ignorant talk of foolish people. Live as free people, but do not use your freedom as a cover-up for evil; live as God's slaves. Show proper respect to everyone, love the family of believers, fear God, honor the emperor.*
>
> *— 1 Pet. 2:11–17*

Ayoung man found himself one day doing something he told himself he would never do. Upon realizing his mistake and knowing in his heart that he wanted to be better, he felt deep fear and despair. Unsettling questions arose in his soul. *How could this be happening?* he thought.

The young man didn't set out to do it. It just happened. In his devastation, he ran as far and as fast as he could until he fell down at last and wept, overcome with shame and embarrassment. Feeling only numbness in his bones and in his spirit, he wondered, *What happens now? After where I've been, God could never love or accept me anymore. He is likely done with me forever.* The young man faintly whispered a prayer for mercy, for that was all he had. *God, help me. I'm so sorry.* And he fell into sleep.

When he awoke, there sitting beside him was the one person he so greatly feared seeing after what he'd done. There, looking intently at him, was Jesus. He felt exposed, raw. Surely, he was condemned. Sheepishly, he looked into Jesus' waiting eyes.

Speaking gently, Jesus said, "I know all about what happened. I saw what you did, and I forgive you. Know this: I will never stop wanting you to be mine. My plans for you haven't changed. My love for you is constant and unchanging. There are things I want you to do for me. Devote your life to feeding and encouraging my sheep. Serve my church. Use your gifts, your energy, your time, your story, and—yes—even your brokenness to show others how good and faithful *I* am."

Hopefully this story awakens you—maybe even softens you a bit—to the reality that behind these words there is a human being with a very human story. That little parable is based on the life of Peter. Peter probably felt something like that after he denied Jesus three times. He fell hard. Jesus found him, forgave him, and then commissioned him for ministry because that's what Jesus does. He rescues, restores, and turns everything around.

> *Only when we reach the end of our resources can he use us mightily.*

Peter goes into his conversation with Jesus—after three denials and a resurrection—broken by sin. He walks away from his conversation with the risen Lord restored by grace, a resurrection all his own, because of God's mercy. This passage in 1 Peter 2 is so compelling, so clear, and so challenging that I want to look at it word for word, line by line.

A Call to Do Hard Things

Everything up to this point has focused on clarifying our identity as the sons and daughters of God and establishing the permanence of our living hope. Peter, in the first chapter, made at least seven statements about identity. Seven times he spoke to who we are in Christ.

In the passage from 1 Peter 2, he asks us to obey Jesus in seven different ways—a fascinating coincidence if you ask me. From the beginning of 1 Peter to verse ten of chapter two, there are thirty explicit statements of encouragement—merely thirty-five verses into his letter, which in total is only five chapters and one hundred and five verses. By the second chapter, there are already thirty words of encouragement and seven affirmations of identity.

I take away two things from those data points. First, the original hearers of his message must have been discouraged and oppressed and afraid. Following Jesus in the first century was a controversial, crazy, and dangerous proposition. Peter knew this. So it makes sense that he would want to encourage and affirm these people as much as he possibly could.

The second reason why I think we have seven identity statements and thirty words of encouragement—in the span of only thirty-five verses—is because he's about to call us to do hard things. An excellent summary of 1 Peter 1:1–2:10 would be this: remember who you are. Beginning in 1 Peter 2:11, the focus is on becoming the person God calls you to be now that you know whose you are and are convinced of what he says about you.

Abstain from Sinful Desires

Verse eleven of chapter two begins the hinge point of 1 Peter:

> Dear friends, I urge you, as foreigners and exiles, to abstain from sinful desires, which wage war against your soul.

Have you ever been around a foreigner before, someone clearly not from your area? Maybe it's their accent, their customs, the food they eat, or the music they listen to that tells you, but somehow you just know. A foreigner is distinct. They stick out. The word "exile" is also an interesting choice of word. An exile is someone being led out either by will or by force from one place to another. They're on a pilgrimage from somewhere they knew well to some other place.

Peter highlights a simple truth about you and me. As followers of Jesus, we live by different rules. We worship a very different Lord. The way we define success, the good life, beauty, and good and evil is often very different than whatever is common in our native territory.

In Philippians 3:20, Paul says, "Our citizenship is in heaven." He doesn't say that it *will be* in heaven but that it *currently is*. The minute you become a follower of Jesus, your citizenship transfer is complete. Now we don't fully come into the blessings of that inheritance—which Peter so eloquently describes in chapter one—but our citizenship is instantly moved. If you are a follower of Jesus, you are first and foremost a citizen of heaven, where God's rule and reign remain unchallenged, and where his worship takes place in every moment. That place is your home.

Peter says that, in light of that reality, we should abstain from evil desires. He could have simply instructed us to stop doing bad things.

He goes for the root, though. Consider whose teaching example he's following there: Jesus', of course. He was personally discipled by Jesus, the most creative and brilliant articulator of inside-out spirituality. Jesus taught that the gospel wasn't about behavior modification. The Pharisees lived as though it was. For them, rules were everything, and it wasn't about becoming a good person. It was about *looking like* a good person, about appearance rather than reality. Their teachings had a rank hypocrisy about them. Their dead religion reflected their dead hope, unfortunately.

Jesus taught that God wants to upend our disordered desires because an ugly part of our sinful nature is that we want many things that are not good for us. Jesus came not only to help us with that reality but to rescue us from it. In him, our desires can become transformed. He gives us the Holy Spirit, not just to help us do better but to help us desire better things. He's going for a heart transformation that is deep and lasting and unmistakable—not mere superficial, short-lived behavior modification. The stakes are immeasurably high.

Did you catch that? These evil desires wage war against you and me. Sounds a bit dramatic, but that's the truth. Peter says there's a war going on in your desires, and the war is against your soul.

You have a soul. You are not only flesh and bone. Part of you—an eternal part of you—has forces inside and outside of your being waging war against you. The forces inflict real harm, with the capability of keeping you from being strong and focused and passionate and pure in your worship of God.

If you're wondering, *What are the sinful desires I should be abstaining from?* only lift your eyes from verse eleven up to verse nine. Just before the hinge of verse eleven, you can find in a clear and wonderful way what your purpose is. As followers of Jesus, we have been called out of darkness and into his light. Once we were not a people, but now we are a people that we may declare the praises of him who has rescued us from sin and death.

We're here for that reason, and so we abstain from any desire that hinders the passionate pursuit of God. It's a pretty sweeping call, admonishing us as God's children to take rigorous, personal inventory of our lives because God desires and demands goodness.

Live Good Lives

Live such good lives among the pagans that, though they accuse you of doing wrong, they may see your good deeds and glorify God on the day he visits us. (1 Pet. 2:12)

"Pagans" is an interesting word not often used. The original word means "Gentiles." In our context, it often refers to people who do not worship the one, true God or acknowledge the exclusive claims of Jesus Christ.

Right there in verse eleven, it says, "Though they accuse you of doing wrong." Well, for us, the accusations are piling up these days, aren't they? Close-minded. Simpletons. Fundamentalists. Hateful. For them, it was far, far worse.

Peter says your life should be so distinct, so inspiring, and so encouraging that people will look at your life and be moved to worship and glorify God. The idea comes from Jesus himself. A living hope runs counterintuitively to life on earth. It's uncanny in an inexplicably attractive way, and that's how others are drawn in. We are to reflect the light of Christ's living hope.

Matthew 5:13 says, "You are the salt of the earth. But if the salt loses its saltiness, how can it be made salty again? It is no longer good for anything, except to be thrown out and trampled underfoot." What was the purpose of salt in the first century? It flavored and preserved food. The whole notion of Christianity being boring is just not true. It's zesty. It's flavorful. Jesus is anything but boring—and a life with him is anything but lifeless and predictable.

Matthew 5 continues:

> You are the light of the world. A town built on a hill cannot be hidden. Neither do people light a lamp and put it under a bowl. They put it on its stand, and it gives light to everybody in the house. In the same way, let your light shine before others, that they may see your good deeds and glorify your father in heaven. (Matt. 5:14–16)

Peter, a disciple of Jesus, is saying the very same thing.

Peter says that our good deeds should be so inspiring that they provoke unbelievers—pagans—to glorify God on the day he visits us. He doesn't explain the phrase "on the day he visits," but I assume he means the day when Christ returns, when all things are made new, and we all bow down—whether we do it willingly or by force—to King Jesus. By heaven's standards, a good life is focused on the kind of person we're becoming. This text demands we ask the question, *Who am I becoming?*

Submit to Human Authority

The ride gets a little bumpier at verse thirteen:

> Submit yourselves for the Lord's sake to every human authority: whether to the emperor, as the supreme authority, or to governors, who are sent by him to punish those who do wrong and to commend those who do right. (1 Pet. 2:13–14)

This verse concerns how followers of Jesus should engage with the government. Peter says that we should submit not for the president's sake nor for the governor's sake but for the Lord's sake. We should see government as a sovereign expression of God's rule.

We've seen political corruption on every level in America. We have witnessed presidents do unspeakable acts of evil and immorality.

We've seen leaders destroy their work, their reputation, and their families because of dishonesty. Haven't we learned by now that sin is no respecter of political position?

The leaders Peter commands his readers to submit to are far worse than anything I've seen in my lifetime. Even a cursory reading about the lifestyle of the Roman emperors would likely cause you to wince. When Peter urged submission to the emperor, he was speaking about a man who could, and would, burn Christians alive or feed them alive to animals.

Peter stated simply that we are to submit to such people. Romans 13 is the clearest passage in the Bible about how we should view government as disciples of Jesus. Paul says:

> Let everyone be subject to the governing authorities, for there is no authority except that which God has established. The authorities that exist have been established by God. Consequently, whoever rebels against the authority is rebelling against what God has instituted, and those who do so will bring judgment on themselves. . . . Therefore, it is necessary to submit to the authorities, not only because of possible punishment but also as a matter of conscience. This is also why you pay taxes, for the authorities are God's servants who give their full time to governing. Give to everyone what you owe them: If you owe taxes, pay taxes; if revenue, then revenue; if respect, then respect; if honor, then honor. (Rom. 13:1–2, 5–6)

Trust that God is overseeing it all. He is the Lord of time. He will bring it to completion when and how he chooses to. We need to trust him in that.

Silence the Talk of Foolish People

> For it is God's will that by doing good you should silence the ignorant talk of foolish people. (1 Pet. 2:15)

People speak in foolish ways about God, and your life should be a redirection of that foolishness. Others should see your life and feel exposed. Our lives should provoke questions, and our actions should be the kind which are quietly noticed and demand some sort of explanation.

Peter says that the silencing of foolish, ignorant talk happens when believers do good things. He doesn't say when we argue effectively, when we speak loudly, or when we trumpet our acts of righteousness to the world. It happens by the way you and I live.

I found myself at a birthday party once with twelve girls under the age of nine. For a few minutes, I was the only man anywhere in sight. The staff? All females. Moms everywhere.

Something surprising and encouraging happened as I was going about the party. Someone who worked at the place we were having the party came up to me and asked if we were Christians. She was seventeen years old, about to be a senior in high school the next year. *That's a weird question*, I thought. *Isn't it just a birthday party?*

I told her we were Christians.

She said, "I knew it," and turned to someone else on staff to say, "I told you."

I thought, *Oh wow, what is that supposed to mean? Were we rude?*

She went on to say that it was the way I welcomed the guests and the way I talked to the kids. I thought, *I didn't know anyone saw any of that.* We were having a birthday party. We had a good day together— and by the grace of God somebody took notice that we were believers.

The conversation really encouraged me because, every now and then, I wonder if I am swimming with the other fishes in our culture. I wonder if the light of Christ truly shines in my life. We didn't do anything heroic. We were nice to people because there's no reason not to be. Kindness is becoming rarer by the day.

> *Jesus invites us to live by a better and truer story.*

We can rest in his finished work on the cross and let his view of us define who we really are. We're free to reject consumerism because the world has nothing to offer to even compare with what we have in Jesus. We can let go of the pride in our own accomplishments because we have been saved only through the grace of God. We have forgiveness and freedom in life, and we didn't give it to ourselves. God gave it to us because he's a God of love and grace. How can you be prideful in the presence of the God of all grace and mercy?

Our past, our present, and our future have all been secured by the Holy Spirit. The minute we came out of the waters of baptism, the Holy Spirit took up residence in us. One day our desires will be finally and fully satisfied. It will be unspeakably glorious. We have been born again into a living hope through the resurrection of Jesus Christ from the dead, into an unperishable, unfading inheritance—an inheritance graciously kept in heaven for us.

Live as Free Slaves

Live as free people, but don't use your freedom as a cover-up for evil; live as God's slaves. (1 Pet. 2:16)

What Peter describes here is one of the great paradoxes and mysteries of the kingdom. We are free slaves. But how does that work exactly? How are we both free and enslaved? How does our surrender to the lordship of Jesus—our enslavement to that truth—free us while the captivities of the world still try to bind us?

Well, obeying Jesus as Lord frees us from the tyranny of other gods. We've been enslaved to God through Christ, specifically through his cross. We are imprisoned by his grace and yet liberated from the bondage of other gods.

Show Respect to Everyone

> Show proper respect to everyone, love the family of believers, fear God, honor the emperor. (1 Pet. 2:17)

How should we treat others, regardless of what they believe, what they look like, where they're from, or what they've done? We should show respect to everyone, always. We need to respect their inherent dignity and worth as sons and daughters of God. This means everyone, no exceptions, no matter where they live, how wealthy or poor they may be, what their job is, what color their skin is, what they struggle with—forget all of that. We are all equally valuable to God, and we are all equally undeserving of God's grace, yet he offers it to us all. Let's respect everyone and teach our children to respect everyone too.

What about the church? "Love the family of believers." Love not the institution but the family of believers. Let love be like a web of discipling relationships, where we say things to each other like this:

> We need to respect everyone's inherent dignity and worth as sons and daughters of God.

- Will you have my back? I'll be there when you need me.
- I'll be present when you feel you might be losing your hope, and I'll let you borrow some of mine.
- When I can't pray anymore, I need you to pray for me.
- When you are struggling in your marriage, you can call me.
- I may not have any answers, but I'll join you in whatever hard place you find yourself.

When you give yourself over to myths and your beliefs begin to stray, it's okay. It's a good thing for someone who knows you and loves you to come with a Bible open and a heart full of the Holy

Spirit saying, "Come back. Come back to the bedrock of your faith. Believe again that God is good. This book can be trusted, and the tomb is empty."

That's what the church, the family of believers, is for. Love them. When you see a member of your church at the store or at the farmers' market, I hope your heart beats a little faster. Not because we're a crazy, creepy cult, but because we're in this life and mission together. Jesus has bound us together. He intended us to be both with each other and for each other. We should love the family of believers with the love of Christ. I long for the day when we stop being cynical about the church and simply love the church, when we stop complaining about the church for not being what we long for and *become* the church we long for.

The church is the bride of Christ, not the preacher's project or the elders' project. God has called preachers and elders to do things in the church to serve you and love you and disciple you. But the church belongs to Jesus. It is his bride. He bought us with his own blood. Let us love the church and love the family of believers.

Fear God

Then in verse seventeen, Peter says, "Fear God."

He lets those two words loose to sink in good and deep: fear God. The fear of God remains a theme in every section of the Bible. Let your fear of God overwhelm your smaller fears—fear of death, fear of unemployment, fear of poverty, fear of rejection, fear of not being liked.

> Let your fear of God quiet those other fears.

Finally, Peter repeats his admonition to honor the emperor, so you know he means it. That urging wasn't easy then and isn't always now;

still, we have a high calling in Christ. He gives us the strength to carry out his calling over us.

Ask for Help

We cannot follow these instructions from Peter on our own. There are things we know are wrong. Our desires are disordered, and they often take us down wrong, destructive roads. We need to ask God for help abstaining from sinful desires. Pray for God to help you reorder your distorted desires, to help you want good things. Some people need to ask God for help honoring the government. Some should ask God for help loving the church as a family of believers.

◆

Lord Jesus, you are a true king. Remind me as we pray, as we ask for help, as we declare our dependence again—remind us that you're here. Lord, we pray for you to restore our broken hearts, our wounded faith. Would you help us to believe that he who began a good work in us will bring it to completion? Take us deeper in prayer. Help us step out behind the charade of pretending to have it all together. Fill us with your living hope. Now, Lord Jesus, by your Spirit and in your name, amen.

Ruthless Trust

A Sermon on 1 Peter 2:18–25

Slaves, in reverent fear of God submit yourselves to your masters, not only to those who are good and considerate, but also to those who are harsh. For it is commendable if someone bears up under the pain of unjust suffering because they are conscious of God. But how is it to your credit if you receive a beating for doing wrong and endure it? But if you suffer for doing good and you endure it, this is commendable before God. To this you were called, because Christ suffered for you, leaving you an example, that you should follow in his steps. "He committed no sin, and no deceit was found in his mouth." When they hurled their insults at him, he did not retaliate; when he suffered, he made no threats. Instead, he entrusted himself to him who judges justly. "He himself bore our sins" in his body on the cross, so that we might die to sins and live for righteousness; "by his wounds you have been healed." For "you were like sheep going astray," but now you have returned to the Shepherd and Overseer of your souls.

— 1 Pet. 2:18–25

The book of 1 Peter offers a clear and helpful answer to a question many of us are asking: What does it mean to trust and follow Jesus in our uncertain, ever-changing, and increasingly anxious world? What does faithfulness to Jesus look like in the present cultural moment?

As I've already established in previous chapters, Peter was uniquely prepared to guide us through that question. Following Jesus in first-century Rome was seen as a strange, outrageous, fledgling, insane movement based on the teachings of a failed, crucified rabbi.

Peter was also uniquely prepared because he was in an inner circle of three men, dearly close brothers and soul friends of Jesus. Jesus invested time and effort into Peter, knowing he would eventually call him to do immensely challenging things. The book of 1 Peter was written nearly thirty years after Jesus was raised from the dead. If you listen carefully enough, you might hear the voice of Jesus coming through every word of 1 Peter 2:18–25.

Peter continued a very intentional sequence of thought in that passage. There's a rationale and a purpose for what he wrote. If all you ever read of Scripture was those eight verses, it would likely be confusing and discouraging. I want to unfold Peter's logic using a grander perspective.

This Is What God Has Done

Peter starts by saying, "This is what God has done." God is greatly merciful. If you have given yourself to him, if he's truly your Lord, then you can say with certainty and confidence that you are born again into a condition—a realm—that Peter describes as living hope. The world is sick with dying hope, hope that will fail, hope that will ultimately disappoint, hope that is not hope at all.

> *What Jesus offers us is living. It's alive, it's in you, and you carry it wherever you go.*

There's more, and it gets better. You have an inheritance—unshakeable, unchangeable, yours—courtesy of the grace of God. This inheritance is not vulnerable or open to attack. It is being kept in heaven right now for you. Through faith you are shielded by God's power until the coming of the salvation that is ready to be revealed. You are currently being shielded by the power of God.

Peter overwhelmed his original readers with good news because they really needed it. As we've already talked about, they were being persecuted and discouraged beyond description, beyond anything we've ever experienced in this life. In terms of corporate persecution for Christianity, what they were going through was unspeakably evil and vile.

Our living hope and promised inheritance do not come from us or because of anything we have done. We didn't create them, nor can we give them to ourselves. At our most spiritual, we can't work up living hope or hold on to our inheritance in our own strength. They come only from Jesus himself, because of his empty tomb, through his resurrection from death.

This Is Who You Are

Peter then moves from "this is what God has done" to "this is who you are." He starts with God and moves from God to us. If you remember from a few chapters ago, we looked at verses nine and ten. We called out seven specific statements Peter makes about our identity in Christ. Those statements are key for understanding who we truly are in Christ.

Identity is a linchpin issue for followers of Jesus. It's not some peripheral thing, and it's not a throwaway thing. We have to know who we are. We must first know what God has done before we can become settled on who we are. With one designation after another, Peter establishes firmly what that identity is:

> You are a chosen people, a royal priesthood, a holy nation, God's special possession, that you may declare the praises of Him who brought you out of darkness into his wonderful light. Once you were not a people, but now you are the people of God; once you had not received mercy, but now you have received mercy. (1 Pet. 2:9–10)

This cluster of verses is laden with Old Testament references and imagery, much of which we unfolded a few chapters before this one. These glorious statements deserve repeating: We don't need priests. We don't need special people or special buildings to gain access to God. Jesus has given us unhindered access.

The moment you give your life to Christ, the Holy Spirit takes up residence in you. You become a walking temple. The Holy Spirit resides within you. You take heaven with you anywhere on earth you go. When people are with you, it is like they are with God because God is in you. That's all strange to say, but we are priests. We are God's special possession. We are owned, operated, and dominated by the authority of God—which is not a threat, but a gift.

Part of our sinful human nature is that we reject all forms of authority—especially the authority of God—as a threat to our independence because we fear being enslaved. Jesus taught that the authority of God was (and is) meant to protect you and help you flourish. It will liberate you from the bondage of self-rule. Jesus came to set you free—mainly from yourself and from the false gods the culture idolizes. That is what God has done. That is who you are.

This Is How You Should Live

Peter declared good news before going on to explain how to follow Jesus, practically speaking. First Peter 1:6–9 says that we should rejoice in the midst of trials, describing a posture of the heart. We walk through trials with joy, not faking it until we make it or complaining because we have been treated unfairly. We walk though trials with a grain of gratitude because we know trials are God's precious gifts. He not only uses us to encourage others in the midst of trials but also shows us how needy and dependent we actually are. Trials come to test the genuineness of our faith and to showcase the unsurpassed greatness of the gospel of Jesus Christ.

In 1 Peter 1:13, Peter says that since this is what God has done and because this is who you are, you should—with a mind that's fully sober—set your hope on the grace to come when Jesus is revealed. He urges us to focus on the second coming of Christ, which is something we really don't do all that often because we have it so good that we rarely think about eternal things. Peter says a follower of Christ should intentionally set their hope—should calibrate their future expectations—according to the riches of heaven, not the pleasures of earth.

In chapter two, Peter encourages us to pursue holiness. It's all throughout the Bible and all throughout 1 Peter: pursue holiness. He says specifically, "Rid yourselves of all malice and all deceit, hypocrisy, envy, and slander of every kind." These are enemies of the heart. We should wage war purposefully, putting to death the old self and letting Jesus resurrect the new self.

Peter is saying that we should be so laser-focused on Jesus, and living in light of what he's done and who we are, that we gladly serve and love our families and others, walk humbly with God, and do good things. We should be so preoccupied with doing those things that the world around us is forced to take notice—not because of what we preach but because of how we live. Living a life of humility and loving even those who don't agree with you, especially about faith and Jesus, will cause those around you to be all the more inspired to worship the one, true God.

The End of Ourselves

Now, these are hard and challenging teachings. They take us to the end of ourselves—the end of our selfishness—and they shatter the prevailing myths of our culture. We can't do any of this without God's help. This is a call for us to say, "I surrender." We can't submit. We can't love. We can't stay quiet. We can't pursue holiness without God's miraculous intervention in our lives, without the people of God walking alongside us.

It is impossible to embrace the lifestyle of trusting and following Jesus alone. It is meant for us to pursue *together.* We fall; we get up. We fall; we get up. We help each other. We encourage each other. We call out the good in each other, and we remind each other of what God has done, who we are, and how we should live.

> The lifestyle of trusting and following Jesus is meant for us to pursue *together.*

Be encouraging. Use your words everywhere you go, with whomever you're around, to remind them of who they are. Remind them even if it's awkward, because you can't over-encourage another disciple.

One time a friend (one of those zany, Spirit-filled guys), while dropping his daughter off at my house, got out of his car and said, "Hey Josh, you conquering, Jesus-filled man of God, you overcomer!" It wasn't awkward. He spoke with genuineness and purpose. When he said those words, funny as they may have sounded, the spirit inside me stood tall because, whether I knew it or not, I needed to hear that. God put those words in my friend's mouth because events happened later in the day to discourage me. But I remembered what my friend had said. It was like he *had* to say it. He *had* to tell me, and it was powerful to hear the truth about me and about who God is.

Our passage for this chapter calls us to a level of ruthless trust that I am often uncomfortable with. We know who God is, and we know what God has done. This is who we are now.

Slaves and Employees

Slave.

Immediately, we want to turn away from that word and everything it represents. We typically read the word "slave" through the lens of the horrible degradation of nineteenth-century slavery in America; however, the situation in Peter's day was far less horrible than what we typically think concerning slavery.

Mistreatment would definitely occur, but servants in that culture generally were well-treated and lived autonomous lives. They were often managers, overseers, and trained members of various professions. They were doctors, nurses, technicians, and skilled artisans. There was extensive Roman legislation around the treatment of servants. Some of them were paid to the point that they could purchase their freedom. Their service *was* involuntary and their legal status, social standing, and opportunity for economic independence *was* clearly lower than others.

Still, a better word to use in understanding this passage and hearing it as it was originally given is probably "employee." So let me rephrase the passage using that word in the place of "slave":

> *Employees, in reverent fear of God, respect the people you work for—not only when they're having a good day and they're treating you fairly, but also when they treat you unfairly. It is commendable when people bear up under pain and they toughen up because they are conscious of God; they're aware of God in the midst of that pain. But if you're treated poorly and you rebel, what good is it? But if you suffer well and you are able to sustain your fear of God through the whole thing, it is not only commendable; it is rare, and it unveils something about God that may not be seen any other way.*

The key point lies in verse nineteen, "being conscious of God"— meaning, bringing an awareness of God into your work, specifically to your relationship with your boss. Now, that's harder for some to hear than others. I don't know who you work for—if you work for yourself, I'll just let you work that out—but this calls us to decompartmentalize our walk with God and instead let that walk become integrated with every part of our lives.

> *How you act and how you engage with and affect others in your workplace is part of your spiritual health.*

An Example of Suffering

To this you were called, because Christ suffered for you, leaving you an example, that you should follow in his steps. "He committed no sin, and no deceit was found in his mouth." When they hurled their insults at him, he did not retaliate; when he suffered, he made no threats. Instead, he entrusted himself to him who judges justly. (1 Pet. 2:21–23)

There's a calling here. You were called, but it isn't a glitzy, shiny, awesome calling. It is a dirty, messy calling that no one wants to bear, with much undeserved suffering. To acknowledge that the earthly authorities we have—governmental or at work—are extensions of the sovereign hand of God, and to honor people and institutions in the name of Jesus with yielded hearts, is a messy, unpopular, and very unattractive calling.

I'm always nervous when people talk about the Christian faith in an overly triumphal, victorious, "high five me in the end zone of life" sort of way. That is not how Jesus called us to live, and it's not reality. Life is hard, and faith is hard. Whoever says otherwise doesn't know what they're talking about, or they are lying to you.

Now, there is joy and power and victory here. By now you must know what a hope junkie I am. This series is called *Living Hope*, but hope wouldn't be hope if pain and hardship didn't exist. Our hope is living because Christ's death-turned-to-life secured our pardon. Even so, the brokenness, sorrow, longing, and suffering precedes the glorious victory.

> Hope wouldn't be hope if pain and hardship didn't exist.

Jesus left us an example of how to suffer. One of the more uncomfortable implications of his example is that we shouldn't be surprised when suffering comes. If Jesus endured it, what makes you think you're so special *not* to endure it? Jesus died on a cross. Peter says he suffered for you. Peter doesn't say he suffered for your forgiveness, although we know he did. He suffered for us to leave an example.

This is where Jesus becomes the most remarkable champion of humanity. He walked through the unspeakable shame and rejection and fear and hardship of the cross, never defending himself, completely sinless. He assumed a non-defensive, non-aggressive posture toward others. He forgave the people who were nailing him to a cross.

If you're like me, you read stuff like this and think, *Well, that's Jesus. I'm not Jesus. Surely, he doesn't really mean for me to follow his example literally.* We begin to let ourselves settle into spiritual mediocrity—or even regression—because we see Jesus as untouchable.

Peter doesn't let us get away with that kind of behavior. He says that Jesus left you an example and you are to follow in his steps, period. If we're following in his steps, that must mean that we're on the same journey he was. It's a journey of suffering and pain and hardship. We shouldn't be surprised when things happen in our families, when people get sick and die, and when life doesn't turn out the way we had planned.

It's easy to be surprised when bad things happen, but when we stop to let the doctrine of sin—and what it means to live in a fallen world—sink in, when we look at the sufferings of Jesus, how can anyone be shocked? We should be more surprised when *good* things happen. If we acknowledge how utterly deserving humanity is of God's wrath, then when good things happen, we should be amazed.

Live for Righteousness' Sake

Peter goes back to the Old Testament with the next verse, to Isaiah 53:9 and 53:6:

> "He himself bore our sins" in his body on the cross, so that we might die to sins and live for righteousness; "by his wounds, you have been healed." (1 Pet. 2:24)

You have been healed from sin—its effects, its power, its penalty, its ultimate consequences. Jesus has healed us not through painless victory, but through suffering and death and sacrifice. Jesus entrusted himself to a greater judge when he was being falsely accused in an illegal trial by ungodly people.

That is what God has done.

Peter continues, "For 'you were like sheep going astray,' but now you have returned to the Shepherd and Overseer of your souls." We were all like sheep, doing our own thing, going our own way, following our own dreams, worshiping false gods, drinking from empty wells. That is who we were, but not who we are.

Who you are now is someone who follows in Christ's steps, someone dead to sin. So, let me ask, how then should you live?

For righteousness.

◆

Father, we give you praise, honor, and glory as the one, true, living God, Creator of heaven and earth, giver of every good and perfect gift. We pray for those who are grieving. We pray for those who are serving in your presence. We honor those who have gone before us. We also ask you, Lord Jesus, by your Holy Spirit that quickens us and awakens us, to blow through this nation like a rushing wind. Would you stir your people to bold, courageous faith? Help us to lean into these anxious times with unshakable confidence in you, our sin-removing, evil-defeating, hope-providing, death-conquering, life-changing Messiah. We embrace this moment, with a heart full of gratitude, as a precious and priceless gift. We pray through Christ, our Lord, amen.

6

A Sacred Covenant

A Sermon on 1 Peter 3:1–7

Wives, in the same way submit yourselves to your own husbands so that, if any of them do not believe the word, they may be won over without words by the behavior of their wives, when they see the purity and reverence of your lives. Your beauty should not come from outward adornment, such as elaborate hairstyles and the wearing of gold jewelry or fine clothes. Rather, it should be that of your inner self, the unfading beauty of a gentle and quiet spirit, which is of great worth in God's sight. For this is the way the holy women of the past who put their hope in God used to adorn themselves. They submitted themselves to their own husbands, like Sarah, who obeyed Abraham and called him her lord. You are her daughters if you do what is right and do not give way to fear. Husbands, in the same way be considerate as you live with your wives, and treat them with respect as the weaker partner and as heirs with you of the gracious gift of life, so that nothing will hinder your prayers.

— 1 Pet. 3:1–7

As we begin 1 Peter 3, we officially enter the main "this is how you should live" section of 1 Peter.

Being told how to live can feel too direct, maybe even controlling. But here Peter is doing us a favor, because following Jesus in a fractured world is a complicated thing—and we need guidance. We need someone to tell us how to live as we are—foreigners and exiles, a strange and peculiar people on earth, people whose citizenship is already in heaven. We need gentle and wise direction as those whose hearts worship the one, true God, who reveals himself perfectly and powerfully in the person and work of Jesus Christ.

In 1 Peter 3:1–7, Peter teaches us about marriage, about how we, as citizens of heaven, should treat our spouses. He speaks directly to wives and then to husbands. I'm not sure who is more challenged or convicted; I'll let you make your own decision about that. But he speaks directly to both sides of the marital coin.

If you're single and thinking, *This is a teaching on marriage, so I can skip it*, know that the principles which govern a Christ-exalting marriage govern every relationship. The principles are transferable. I'm sure you already see that. Ask God to help you navigate your own life circumstances, and trust that he'll be faithful.

Before we dig into this, let me remind you of something I hope you already know. The hard calling God has for you is preceded by God's gracious posture toward you. So the hard things God is calling you to do—the challenging and courageous decisions the Lord asks of you—are preceded by his extravagant grace poured out for you.

To Wives

> Wives, in the same way submit yourselves to your own husbands so that, if any of them do not believe the word, they may be won over without words by the behavior of their wives, when they see the purity and reverence of your lives. Your beauty should not come from outward adornment, such as elaborate hairstyles and the wearing of gold jewelry or fine

clothes. Rather, it should be that of your inner self, the unfading beauty of a gentle and quiet spirit, which is of great worth in God's sight. (1 Pet. 3:1–4)

Verse one begins with "in the same way." Peter was continuing the theme from earlier concerning submission. He had already called his readers to embrace a submissive posture toward authorities in their government and workplace. Peter said that submission is a trademark of all Jesus-honoring relationships. It's not just for wives and husbands but for every Christian, in every relationship.

He said that wives should submit to their husband's leadership in marriage. The concept is often confusing and even offensive to many people in our culture. However, when you submit to somebody else, it does not mean you are inferior or less valuable than they are. This teaching has nothing, absolutely nothing, to do with dignity or worth. The command for wives to submit to their husbands should never, ever be taken to imply inferior personhood and importance or lesser spirituality. Nothing could be further from the truth. Peter affirms the opposite, and the life of Jesus affirms the opposite.

Common Submission

Submission is the hallmark of every great marriage. Show me a marriage where there is no submission, and it won't be much of a relationship. There will be very little closeness, joy, and intimacy. It will feel more like an arrangement than a marriage. In Ephesians 5:21, the apostle Paul says that husbands and wives should submit to each other out of their common submission to Jesus—meaning mutual submission.

> Submission is the hallmark of every great marriage.

Two people loving and deferring to one another and sacrificing for each other is the bedrock of marriage.

Here Peter is talking specifically to wives. The word he uses for submission is *hypotassō*, which always implies a submissive relationship to an authority. It is used elsewhere in the New Testament to talk about Jesus submitting to his parents, demons being subject to disciples, citizens being subject to the governing authorities, unseen spiritual powers being subject to Christ, and Jesus being subject to God the Father. All those relationships utilize the same word and same idea.

The same word is used for church members submitting to church leaders and, here in 1 Peter, wives being subject to their husbands. Here's the thing: none of these relationships ever get reversed, which is good news. This is not a word of oppression, and this is not a word of bondage. It is a good, wise, and timely word. Marriage is an analogy for the relationship that Jesus has with his people. That relationship can never be reversed. Jesus will never submit to the church, and the church can never provide for and protect Jesus the way he provides for and protects his church. It's countercultural. It's controversial. But it's God's plan for us and for our flourishing.

To Husbands

In verse seven, Peter talks to husbands:

> Husbands, in the same way be considerate as you live with your wives, and treat them with respect as the weaker partner and as heirs with you of the gracious gift of life, so that nothing will hinder your prayers. (1 Pet. 3:7)

"In the same way" shows back up again. He tells husbands to be considerate, not to think about their own self or interests but to consider their wives, be aware of them, see them, and observe their unique desires and frustrations.

Wives are joint heirs of God's grace. They are equally valuable to God. Even though husbands bear the burden of leadership in the home, wives are equally valued and loved by God. The last verse is absolutely sobering. Peter says that if husbands fail to love their wives, well, we can expect our prayers to be hindered.

There's a link between how we husbands treat our wives and the way God responds to our prayers. It's right there. Peter doesn't drag it out. He just leaves it there on the page and moves on. It should send a shockwave into the soul of every husband who reads it, including me.

An Interview with Tony and Kathy

I thought it would be encouraging and enlightening if I shared wisdom from another couple about what 1 Peter 3:1–7 looks like in marriage. Tony and Kathy Dupree have been married since 1969. Tony is an elder in my church and a gifted Bible teacher. Kathy is sharp and steady and wise. I can't imagine my life, my family, or my church without Tony and Kathy. The following is an interview I held with them about this passage.

Tony: We are certainly not the perfect marriage. We've made a lot of mistakes. About a month ago, Kathy and I were just talking about how we are getting older. I said, "You know, Kathy, maybe someday I'll have to go into assisted living." She looked at me and said, "You've been in assisted living for fifty years." And you know, I really didn't have an answer for that.

Kathy: Our story begins almost fifty-five years ago. We were married young. Tony was twenty-one; I was twenty.

In about the eleventh or twelfth year of our marriage, Tony was moving up the corporate ladder. We had three little children; the twins were five, and our youngest was four. Life had not turned out like I thought it was going to be. It was hard. I had developed a lot of anger, a lot of resentment, and a lot of perfectionism. I was trying to be Martha Stewart, and it wasn't working very well.

At one point, someone in the neighborhood invited me to a baby shower. I went. I was very lonely, and at the baby shower, the people were so nice. I thought, *What's with these women?* There was something different about them, but I really did not know what it was. Two weeks later this woman invited me to a Bible study, and I thought, *Whoa, I don't think I want to do that.* I grew up in church, until the day we got married, when I said I wasn't going ever again. Before that, I was there Sunday morning, Sunday night, and Wednesday night. When this woman asked me, I really did not want to go. But they said they had good coffee, so I went.

But before going I told Tony, because I figured he would say, "Don't go." And instead he said, "Can't hurt." We were going different directions at ninety miles an hour. Remember, I had that anger problem. What he said really made me mad, but I went to the Bible study anyway.

We were studying in 1 John about how God loves us. I understood that Jesus died for the sins of the whole world. I got that part, but I never understood until that Bible study that my sins of anger, resentment, and all those things that I was dealing with put Jesus on the cross. I came to Jesus and asked him to take over my life. I was born again. Tony wanted me to go to this Bible study, so I thought, *Well, I'll just do my lessons out loud. He needs to know this too.* This was a huge turning point in our family.

Tony: Kathy's story really ties into 1 Peter 3, where it says, "Wives, in the same way, submit yourselves to your own husbands so that, if any of them do not believe the word"—that was me—"they may be won over without words by the behavior of their wives."

I was kind of like Kathy. I grew up in a church, but I never really had a personal relationship with Jesus. We were twelve years into our marriage, and Kathy had these anger issues. All of a sudden, she came home, and we started studying those lessons. I really wasn't interested though.

But you know what got me? Kathy really was a different person. Suddenly she was gentle and kind, and I thought, *Who is this woman I'm living with?* It was her behavior that softened my heart enough to think that something real was going on.

So I began to study Scripture, and about a year later I was baptized into Christ. So, to a large extent, I was won over without words by the behavior of my wife, just like the text says. She came to the Lord, and her transformation drew me in.

Roles and Responsibilities in Marriage

> I was won over without words by the behavior of my wife.

Josh: So this text speaks of the different roles in marriage. I think there's a lot of pressure in our culture to say that men and women in the marriage have identical roles and responsibilities. There's no gender differentiation. It doesn't exist. It's a myth. It's old-fashioned. Kathy, I would love to hear you talk about what submission has looked like in your marriage.

Kathy: Well, when we got married, I had no clue about submission. I am very independent. I like to be in control. I have an opinion about probably everything. Submission has been very difficult for me. Tony and I mostly agree on everything, but once in a while, we don't. We had a submission issue this morning about which side of the church to sit on. He won.

Josh: Let me ask you this, Kathy. The word "submit" triggers people and has all manner of weird, negative connotations. How has submission been a blessing? How have you seen God's goodness and God's wisdom through submission?

Kathy: Well, it really is God's way of protection. God never asks us to do anything not ultimately for our benefit. He never calls us to do anything that is sin. If we ignore God's plan, we only hurt ourselves. I am very comforted to know that I am under God's protection. I'm under Tony's umbrella of protection as well. There's freedom in that. There's peace. It's just the way it should be, and it's really good.

Josh: What would you advise ladies, especially those who may be pushing back on the idea of submission to husbands?

Kathy: Well, it's a command. It says to submit to your husbands. We're really submitting to Jesus in that. We're trusting and following him, believing that he's going to take care of us. He's going to protect and lead us. Your husband and your family should be the number one benefactors of your life.

Attitude is so important. It is a choice that we make. A wise woman told me many, many years ago, "What's in the well comes up in the bucket." If you are harboring resentment, anger, or jealousy, whatever it is, it will come out if that's what's in your heart.

Josh: Tony, how has your connection with Jesus affected how you see and treat Kathy?

Tony: When I first became a believer, it really changed our marriage. I started reading the Bible. I began to take my role as a spiritual leader seriously because the Bible talks about the authority a husband has. I've learned, as you mentioned today, that there's authority and submission. It's in the military, and I saw it in the business world. The whole world is set up that way. But with authority comes responsibility, and it really changed how I looked at our marriage.

Husbands, you're primarily responsible for the spiritual health of your family. I remember when I first started reading the Bible in Genesis. When this all started, I didn't know anything about the Bible, and it was interesting to me that when Eve ate the fruit, God went looking for Adam. It always struck me. I think the real first sin was that Adam failed to lead and protect his wife and family.

Clinging to the Promise

Tony: I think the key is a commitment to covenant, to being promise keepers. I read an article years ago; I remember the title: "A Promise Spoken and Not Forgotten." It went on to talk about our marriage vows. When they say, "For better or for worse," they mean what they say. "Till death do us part" means what it says.

Sometimes there are hard times in your marriage. It doesn't mean "until you stop meeting my needs" or "until I don't love you anymore." It doesn't mean "until someone better comes along." Covenant is so important because feelings are not a good foundation for a lifelong relationship. They're important, but it must be a covenant.

I mean, when we first fell in love, I was in a rock band. She was a groupie. And now look at us. The point is, you hear people say that their spouse isn't the same person they married. Of course not. We're changing and growing all the time. I can't tell you how different we are as people. You get married, and you're young, and whether you've been married a year or fifty, you start off as soulmates. But then life hits and things change. One person starts growing at a different rate. One person's interests move, and then the kids come, and then the career, and then teenagers, and it just goes on and on and on.

When Kathy first went to that Bible study, divorce was right there at the door, and God saved us from that. But as we lived another forty years into this, as we marched along, I saw that as we've moved and changed, the thing that has tethered us and brought us back together again and again is our covenant—a promise spoken and not forgotten.

Kathy: As wives, we really need to find out what pleases our husbands. Little things matter a lot. You know what those things are. Spend time together. Take weekends away without the children. Go out for dinner without the kids. It's very, very important to keep your relationship maintained and keep communication going.

Josh: Tony, I want to address that last verse. It seems to indicate that a husband's connection with God and our treatment of our wives are related to each other. I would love for you to just ruminate and exhort us as husbands with verse seven.

Tony: We need to be listening and obeying whatever God tells us to do. This verse is totally independent of whether Kathy is submitting or not, and her submission is not dependent on whether I'm loving her as Christ loved the church. Sometimes I'm not very loving, but she still has a responsibility. Sometimes she doesn't submit so well, sometimes maybe her role gets off track, but I still have to love her.

What Does it Look Like to Cherish?

Tony: God speaks to the husbands. The text says, "In the same way be considerate as you live with your wives" (1 Pet. 3:7)—meaning, dwell with your wife according to knowledge and understanding. It's not talking about physically living with her but understanding our wives' goals and frustrations. What is she afraid of? What brings her fear? What brings her joy?

Kathy: I'm going to tell a little story about something Tony did very well. Life has not always been easy for us. We've had ups and downs. We've had victories. We've had joys, but we've gone through tough things together.

We had been married about twenty years, and my mom came to live with us. She had struggled with depression and health issues most of her life. But she came to live with us, and we were consumed by her. We had three teenagers. After about six months with us, she decided to overdose on antidepressants and took her own life. It was very, very difficult, and I had to be so strong for the family, just keeping everybody together.

The day of her funeral, I went in to get dressed. Finding clothes has never been a problem for me, but that day I could not even pick out an outfit. Tony came in and said, "Wear this. I know you look nice in it." That was huge for me.

Tony: You know what's interesting? I don't even remember that. I will say this particularly to the husbands: Your wife will remember those little things even if you don't.

The text talks about treating your wife with respect as the weaker partner. We can spend a lot of time on that verse, but really at the heart of it is to care for and cherish your wife as something of great value.

Then Peter talks about how we are going to be coheirs. You see that we all have roles to play in our lives. In marriage, we have roles to play as well. What Peter is reminding us—and what the Bible says again and again in terms of value and worth before God—is that we're in this together. We're partners. We're not competitors. Our goal is to help each other trust and follow Jesus as best we can.

Much of what we're talking about today is so contrary—so politically incorrect—to our culture and to the sector of the world we live in. But after fifty years, I know a thing or two, because I've seen a thing or two. God's ways work because he made us and established marriage, and if we follow his plan—even with all of our flaws—God will bless it.

Kathy: You absolutely cannot do this on your own.

As Christians, we have the Holy Spirit to hold us up through difficulties, through good times and through bad times. The Holy Spirit teaches us, convicts us, and convinces us. He strengthens us. He gives us victory. And that's true whether you're married or single.

◆

Lord Jesus, thank you for speaking so powerfully and clearly through Kathy and Tony and through 1 Peter 3:1–7. Help us to submit to your wisdom; help us cast away the voices contradicting your wisdom. Help us ruthlessly trust in Jesus. We fix our eyes on you. Help us, Lord Jesus. Give us strength, wisdom, hope, and grace. Amen.

Strengthened for Suffering

A Sermon on 1 Peter 3:15–22

> *But in your hearts revere Christ as Lord. Always be prepared to give an answer to everyone who asks you to give the reason for the hope that you have. But do this with gentleness and respect, keeping a clear conscience, so that those who speak maliciously against your good behavior in Christ may be ashamed of their slander. For it is better, if it is God's will, to suffer for doing good than for doing evil. For Christ also suffered once for sins, the righteous for the unrighteous, to bring you to God. He was put to death in the body but made alive in the Spirit. After being made alive, he went and made proclamation to the imprisoned spirits—to those who were disobedient long ago when God waited patiently in the days of Noah while the ark was being built. In it only a few people, eight in all, were saved through water, and this water symbolizes baptism that now saves you also—not the removal of dirt from the body but the pledge of a clear conscience toward God. It saves you by the resurrection of Jesus Christ, who has gone into heaven and is at God's right hand—with angels, authorities and powers in submission to him.*
>
> *— 1 Pet. 3:15–22*

Who can say they've never been on the receiving end of the grace and power and mercy of Jesus? His mercies are new every morning. The core conviction of discipleship is found in 1 Peter 3:15. It's the heart cry of the life of a disciple. The governing idea of this whole passage is verse fifteen: "In your hearts revere Christ as Lord." The English Standard Version translates it this way: "In your hearts honor Christ the Lord as holy." Jesus has earned our trust, has he not? He has shown us his faithfulness in countless ways, especially in his death and resurrection. We've looked to Jesus. We're astounded by his wisdom. We're blown away by his power. We're overjoyed by the grace he gives us every day. We're grateful for the ongoing work of redemption in our lives. We experience his renewing power day in and day out, whether we feel that power or not.

Jesus has done more than enough to earn our trust. In our hearts, in the deepest parts of us, we surrender to him as Lord, and we give him access to every part of our lives, especially the areas we're most reluctant to turn over to him. This is more than just an intellectual belief. It's more than just fascination. It's a heartfelt conviction that drives us to live with what Peter calls "living hope."

The original recipients and hearers of Peter's letter were hungry for hope. They faced rejection, persecution, violence, and death at the hands of a tyrannical, pagan government. And the world is still longing for hope. Too often we are faced with a new crisis. It's overwhelming to hear of what's happening all over the world.

Nationally, we have a political climate that seems to be increasingly tense, dramatic, and hostile. We have, it seems, innumerable crises just in our own country, not to mention in every state and every city. Looking in on your home and your family, is it perfect and drama free? Is it easy? Are there any challenges going on? Moving in even closer, look at your own individual life and the struggles you deal with. It is overwhelming to live in a sin-dominated world, mortally wounded by evil.

Peter would say you can have hope during it all, no matter how hard or impossible it may seem. The way to get this hope is to revere Jesus as Lord in your heart, day by day. Jesus is the only true and legitimate pathway to living hope.

An Explanation Demanded

The hope he gives is like a flame that can never be put out. It is untouchable, indestructible. It is resilient and glorious. It makes us shine like stars in the sky. In fact, in many cases, Christian hope is so distinct and so otherworldly that it often demands an explanation.

Verse fifteen says, "Always be prepared to give an answer to everyone who asks you to give the reason for the hope that you have." The phrase "give an answer" literally means to make a defense. It's where we get the word "apologetics." It envisions a scenario in which we're responding to a question. In this case, Peter must be assuming that the inward hope of Jesus' followers results in lives that are very different from those who don't follow Jesus. Our lives should be so noticeably different that they prompt questions. So be prepared to give the reason for the hope that you have.

How exactly can others witness our hope? Hope is invisible. By definition, you can't see hope, as it is not a tangible reality. Well, Peter gives us a strong contextual clue in verses thirteen and fourteen:

> Who is going to harm you if you are eager to do good? But even if you should suffer for what is right, you are blessed. Do not fear their threats; do not be frightened. (1 Pet. 3:13–14)

The reason people, specifically unbelievers, would ask about our hope without our slamming it down their throat, the reason they would initiate a conversation about hope, is because they see in us a strange and peculiar fearlessness. Or maybe a better way to put it is this:

> They see that we aren't controlled by the same
> fears they are, and our absence of fear is striking.

Once when I was at the Vanderbilt-Ingram Cancer Center getting chemo, I had an interesting hope-explanation encounter. I could tell early on that it was going to be a long day, and I knew I had two options: I could either partner with God and bless people, or I could go crazy. I chose to partner with God that day, by his grace.

I saw her right by the elevator. She was in her mid-to-late fifties, with graying hair at the temples, and she was shaking. She was crying, but she didn't look sick. I went to my seat, opened my laptop, and started writing and reading and doing what I do. I felt a strange prompting: *You may need to talk to her. This may be the open door to encourage somebody you've prayed for.* But I didn't want to force it. I didn't want to be the guy to go over to a crying woman and say, "Are you okay?" Clearly, she was not. I didn't want to have a weird, forced conversation.

I went inside the restroom to wash my hands, and I said to God, "If you want me to talk to this lady, then I want to know it." When I came out of the restroom, she had wheeled her husband over, and they were now sitting right beside me.

He was not doing so well physically. He was there, and he was struggling. She had half a dozen bags around her, full of notebooks, pillows, cups, and food. I started chatting with them, asking how the day was going. The moment I said something to her, she started crying uncontrollably.

She said finally, "My distractions aren't working."

I asked, "What do you mean?"

She said, as she was pulling stuff out of her bag, "I brought all this stuff with me. I'm the bag lady." She had books, her laptop, her iPad, her phone, some scrapbooks, and some work materials. She said, "This is not happening to us. I can't be here anymore. The only way I know how to get through this is to be distracted."

I thought, *I can either tell her in this moment, "Well, Jesus is the answer to this," or I can get in the ditch with her and say, "You know, I've been there. I know what this feels like, and it's really hard."*

I chose to go down that latter road with her. At the end of our conversation, she said, "Has anybody ever asked you about your hope?"

Now I ask you: Has anybody ever asked you that? Have you ever had to explain why you don't overreact to life?

Our posture of non-anxious trust in God is provocative. It is attractive. We are free from being troubled thanks to God's grace and the power of the Holy Spirit that raised Jesus from the dead. We are—day by day, moment by moment—outgrowing fear. In him, we are able to live with a non-reactive spirit, and this is confusing to most people. We're not afraid of the same things they're afraid of.

What does the world put their hope in? Most often it is safety, comfort, money, acceptance, or health. What about the followers of Jesus? Where's our hope? Our hope is fixed on a person who has overcome death. He has defeated every enemy. Sickness? He beat that one. Water? He walked on it. Blindness? Conquered that. Every time he encountered an evil spirit or a demon, he was able to cast it out. Religious persecution? Hypocrisy? He was able to kick those into the darkness and expose them as inauthentic. People were coming against Jesus left and right, but he could not be defeated.

The last enemy is death. Jesus emerged from the grave. When people put their hope in and bet the farm on the resurrection of Jesus, the way they engage with fear is completely altered. It changes everything. We cling to hope in the middle of the mess, and that doesn't make sense—but for Jesus. Our souls know that it is indeed in him that we live and move and have our being, so we trust and strive to follow him. We have a living hope because we have experienced the goodness of God on earth—despite the suffering, despite the troubles, despite living so far removed from the actual events of Christ's resurrection.

But our tone should be humble when somebody does say to us, "Why aren't you freaking out right now? Why aren't you anxious? Because from where I'm standing, you have reasons to be anxious." There's no room for pride because we didn't do anything; Jesus did.

Preparing for Pain

It's clear that the main point of this passage is to help us get ready to suffer, not for doing what is wrong but for doing what is right. If you look at the big picture of this passage, it is all about preparation for pain.

We can't forget the main point: Peter is arming us with faith. We need to suffer. Nothing reveals the glory and the reality of God like a believer who suffers. We live in a culture of pain avoidance. We will do anything and everything we can to avoid pain—shortcuts, eject buttons, numbing agents, anything to opt out of pain.

In the Bible, pain is a portal through which God enters our lives and shows us uncomfortable things. Pain is the open door through which God transforms our character and teaches us. Trials are essential for transformation. Acts 14 says that we must go through many hardships to enter the kingdom of God. So, as Peter says, suffering is inevitable. Pain will come when it comes, so we would be wise to get ready.

> Pain is a portal through which God enters our lives.

Peter gives us four truths to help us when pain inevitably comes, each one beautiful and glorious in its own right. If you're in a season of suffering and pain right now, I hope your heart receives these truths like a sponge. If you're in a place of peace and joy, and pain is far away, tuck these truths away for when you'll need them.

1. Remember What Jesus' Suffering Accomplished

The first thing Peter reminds us as we prepare to suffer is to remember what Jesus' suffering accomplished for us. Peter strengthens us to suffer by telling us that Jesus has triumphed over our greatest enemy and brought us safely to God.

Some might wonder why anyone would become a follower of Jesus if things would probably go worse for them in this life and their lives would be at risk. Well in answer to that, the Bible shows that the greatest human needs are not to live long on the earth and to be comfortable, healthy, wealthy, and wise. Those are not the ways of God.

Our greatest, deepest, most pressing human need is to have our sins forgiven, to overcome our separation from God, and to live forever with joy in his presence—which is what the death of Jesus accomplished for us. Verse eighteen says, "Christ also suffered once for sins, the righteous for the unrighteous, to bring you to God."

Notice these four things from that one verse:

Christ died for our sins. Sin is what separates us from God. Our biggest need is to become unseparated. Our biggest enemy is Satan. Isaiah 59:2 says, "Your iniquities have made a separation between you and your God" (NASB). That is way more terrifying than suffering for righteousness' sake. Suffering the wrath of God because sins have not been forgiven is the scariest thing in the world. But Jesus died for our sins. I do not have to die in my sins. There is forgiveness. That is such good news.

Jesus died, the righteous for the unrighteous. His death was a substitution for ours. He took our place. He stood under the wrath of God and the penalty we deserved, and he took it from us. This should produce in us a gratitude so big that it's unexplainable. His death was innocent. It was all for other people and not for himself.

Jesus died once for all. It was sufficient to accomplish the forgiveness of all who put their faith in him. He does not have to ever offer another sacrifice. It is finished. It was all that's necessary to take away the guilt of our sins. The debt has been paid in full.

We are reconciled back to God. His sacrifice brings us to God. If I can be totally honest with you, in my own trials this has been my greatest comfort:

> The reconciliation I most desperately long for with my Father in heaven has already been accomplished because of what Jesus has done.

Our worst enemy, sin, has been defeated, and Jesus has made sure that we will be safe at home with God. He has brought us to God. The separation has been removed. God is near us and for us and in us. My life is now hidden with Christ in God.

How does that help us suffer well? Here's why: One of the greatest and most terrifying temptations of the devil is to make us think God has abandoned us. What Peter says here is that suffering for the believer is not a sign that God has forsaken us and turned against us. Jesus has carried our sins away and brought us safely to God.

We serve a God who suffers with us and will leverage our suffering for our ultimate good.

2. Remember Noah

Remember what happened in Noah's day?

> After being made alive, he went and made proclamation to the imprisoned spirits—to those who were disobedient long ago when God waited patiently in the days of Noah while the ark was being built. In it only a few people, eight in all, were saved through water. (1 Pet. 3:19–20)

There's a lot of controversy over what that refers to. I'll tell you what I think it is and how it relates to this topic. I think it refers to the disobedience of people in Noah's day. The story can be found in

Genesis 6. People ridiculed Noah as a righteous man obeying God. They said he was crazy. But he was obeying God—doing what God explicitly told him to do, in exactly the way God told him to do it.

Peter's readers would have been in a similar situation to Noah as far as ridicule. They faced amazing and harsh opposition from the outside culture. What I think this passage is saying is that Jesus was sent by God in those days to preach to those people through Noah. Just like it says in 1 Peter 1:11, the spirit of Jesus was in the Old Testament prophets, predicting his coming. So the spirit of Jesus was in Noah, preaching to the disobedient people of Noah's day.

The text says that the spirits are now in prison, a place of torment and punishment, awaiting the final judgment. I don't think this verse refers to Jesus going to the realm of the dead and preaching to the spirits there. I understand it to mean that Jesus went to preach in the days of Noah to people who, because they rejected that preaching, are now in prison awaiting the final judgment.

Now, what does that have to do with anything, much less our lives here and now? Well, it strengthens us for suffering in three ways:

It assures us of the greatness of Jesus. He is not bound by space and time. He was there preaching thousands of years before, and he is here today. He will be with you, as he said at the end of his earthly ministry in Matthew 28, to the end of the age. In China and Ireland and Uganda and Israel and Belarus—wherever you may suffer, both now and forever, Jesus will be there.

It is better to obey him. It is better to obey him and suffer than to disobey him and be thrown into the prison of verse nineteen. That's what happened to those spirits in Noah's day. They thought it was foolish to heed the call of God like Noah was doing, so they stayed comfortable and prideful until the rain started to fall. Only then did their hearts change, but it was far too late.

We should not worry about being a minority. We really need to hear this. We should not worry about being a small, rejected minority. That's our reality. It's always been the reality of God's people. That is the point of verse twenty, where it describes how eight persons were brought safely through the water in the ark.

It may have felt foolish to be in such a small group, but the point is this: if you are in a minority with God, you will be saved. When the tables turn, when suffering comes, don't assume the story has changed. Nothing has changed. Only trust God, and hold on, and let God be God.

3. Remember What God Did Through Baptism

The third way Peter encourages us to suffer is in reminding us of what God did when we were baptized. He links the flood account of Genesis 6 to being baptized into Christ. The flood waters that brought judgment on the world in Noah's day remind us of our own baptism:

> This water symbolizes baptism that now saves you also—not the removal of dirt from the body but the pledge of a clear conscience toward God. (1 Pet. 3:21)

It saves you by the resurrection of Jesus Christ. Verse eighteen says that Jesus died for sins and brought us to God. What's clear in this passage is that the people whom Jesus' death actually saves—in verse twenty-one—are those who have been baptized. Peter knows this will be misunderstood if he doesn't qualify it, so he says that "baptism now saves you."

Then he adds further, "It is not about the removal of dirt." Baptism is about appealing to God for cleansing, but not cleansing of the body. Baptism is a way of saying to God, "I trust you to apply the spectacular benefits of Jesus' death to me, and to bring me through death and through judgment for my sins into eternal life, through the resurrection of Jesus." This is the strongest and clearest definition of baptism. It is an appeal for God to cleanse us. Baptism may clean the body, but it saves our souls because it is an expression of faith in Jesus. We are saved by grace through faith. Baptism is an expression of faith.

So how does this strengthen us for suffering? When we have come through the waters of baptism, we have passed through death and through judgment, and we can say that death and judgment are now in the rearview mirror. We have been buried with Jesus and been raised with him. We've passed from death into life, left judgment behind, and moved beyond the suffering we may be experiencing right now.

It may be bad. It may be hard. It may feel impossible at times, but it is nothing compared to the weight and the pain of ongoing condemnation at the hands of a holy God—a condemnation already experienced by Jesus on our behalf. We have received it by faith, and we have expressed that faith in baptism. Our baptism stands as a constant reminder that the worst suffering has already been averted. Jesus took it, and there is now no condemnation. We have already died that death in Christ, and we have already been raised with him.

Therefore, our present suffering is not the wrath of God. It is the loving discipline of our Father, and it is only greater preparation for glory.

4. Remember That Jesus Reigns Supreme

Peter says Jesus "has gone into heaven and is at God's right hand—with angels, authorities and powers in submission to him" (1 Pet. 3:22). Take this one thought with you as you prepare for your own suffering, or even as you suffer. All angels, authorities, powers, devils, evil spirits, and Satan himself are subject to Jesus. All authority in heaven and on earth has been given to Jesus.

When Peter says at the end of the letter that the devil prowls around like a roaring lion, seeking somebody to devour, and to resist him in your faith—this is the faith he has in mind. This is the faith of verse twenty-two, the faith that has all angels, authorities, and powers subject to King Jesus. This is what we rebuke and resist the devil with.

Romans 8:28 is still in the Bible: "We know that in all things God works for the good of those who love him." If you love God, if you've given your life to Jesus, then Satan may come for you. He may attack you, stealing, killing, and destroying things that are precious to you. But every single attack will be turned into your ultimate good on that final day. And you can say that to his face and suffer well because Jesus has been given all authority.

> None of this removes our pain. But it reframes and redeems it.

It's good news. It doesn't remove our pain. None of this removes our pain, but it does reframe and redeem it. The sufferings we endure in this life will pale in comparison to the glory that will be revealed in the next life.

Jesus, thank you for your Word. We praise you for the truths that set us free. We lift you up as the sovereign ruler over all things in heaven and on earth. Sometimes it's hard to believe that because life can be brutal here. Now we ask you to help us believe in the gospel all the way—the good news that you have died for our sins, have been raised from the dead, and have given us the Holy Spirit. Help us to believe your promises are true, and that you are infinitely wise and gloriously trustworthy. Speak to our hearts and strengthen us for suffering. We pray in your name, amen.

8

Walking Through the Fire

A Sermon on 1 Peter 4:12–19

Dear friends, do not be surprised at the fiery ordeal that has come on you to test you, as though something strange were happening to you. But rejoice inasmuch as you participate in the sufferings of Christ, so that you may be overjoyed when his glory is revealed. If you are insulted because of the name of Christ, you are blessed, for the Spirit of glory and of God rests on you. If you suffer, it should not be as a murderer or thief or any other kind of criminal, or even as a meddler. However, if you suffer as a Christian, do not be ashamed, but praise God that you bear that name. For it is time for judgment to begin with God's household; and if it begins with us, what will the outcome be for those who do not obey the gospel of God? And, "If it is hard for the righteous to be saved, what will become of the ungodly and the sinner?" So then, those who suffer according to God's will should commit themselves to their faithful Creator and continue to do good.

— 1 Pet. 4:12–19

This passage begins by talking about the fiery ordeals which sweep into our lives to test us. What are these exactly? Peter wrote to first-century early believers in Rome. It could be that he saw the horrible persecution of Nero coming, where Christians were burned alive.

But I think it may be better understood by looking to a parallel passage in 1 Peter, where the words "fire" and "test" came up previously:

> In all this you greatly rejoice, though now for a little while you may have had to suffer grief in all kinds of trials. These have come so that the proven genuineness of your faith—of greater worth than gold, which perishes even though refined by fire—may result in praise, glory and honor when Jesus Christ is revealed. (1 Pet. 1:6–7)

So here we have fiery trials, and instead of referring to one terrible thing, verse six simply describes them as "all kinds of trials." If you look for examples of the trials themselves in 1 Peter, they range from beatings to verbal abuse:

> How is it to your credit if you receive a beating for doing wrong and endure it? But if you suffer for doing good and you endure it, this is commendable before God. To this you were called, because Jesus suffered for you, leaving you an example that you should follow in his steps. (1 Pet. 2:20–21)

There's the trial of being insulted in 1 Peter 3:9, the trial of being slandered in 3:16, and then in 4:4, there's the trial of being maligned for not living the way you used to—in reckless, godless living.

I think we would do well not to interpret the fiery trial of 1 Peter 4:12 too narrowly. The trials of 1 Peter include being beaten, insulted, slandered, and verbally abused, not to mention that the sufferings of Christ stand before us as a summary of what we can expect as his followers.

Prosperity Promises

Let me warn you about believing promises of prosperity. For those of us leaning into the truth of God's word, suffering in one manner or another is something we expect. We praise God for our blessings, and we turn to him in our troubles. That's what walking with God is. But if we are not vigilant, the prosperity gospel can sneak in during times of overwhelming trial or suffering.

Prosperity gospel is a false and destructive belief. Many of us were raised in it. The concept exists on a spectrum; it's not just one church or denomination. It shows itself in outlandish and glamorous ways and in more subtle ways. Most simply put, if a person does good things, God will reward them with a luxurious and pain-free life. As if the God of all creation is under obligation to give you a blessed life. Not to mention, we often define blessing very differently than Jesus would.

I don't know whether this has been an issue for you. I can't speak intelligently about what you face. But I hear this insidious, dark belief creep up in a myriad of ways when I listen to others talk about how we respond to suffering and trials. I'll talk more about that later in this chapter. Living hope doesn't mean a better life on earth; it means a life on earth with the knowledge that eternal life awaits.

In the remaining verses of the passage, Peter encourages us to respond to fiery ordeals in five specific ways. As we go through these, ask God to help you and strengthen you. There is incredible wisdom to be found here, and in order for us to live it out, we need God's power.

1. Don't Be Surprised

> Don't be surprised at the fiery ordeal that has come upon you to test you as though something strange were happening. (1 Pet. 4:12)

Why are fiery ordeals not strange in the life of a disciple of Jesus? Because in God's wisdom, he planned for the sufferings of Jesus to save us from the sufferings of punishment—not from the sufferings of purification. Read that one more time:

> The sufferings of Jesus save us and rescue us from the suffering of punishment and ultimate condemnation, but they do not protect us from the suffering of purification.

They save us from the fires of judgment but not the fire of refining.

In fact, in 1 Peter 1:7 we're told that, far from being strange and surprising in God's plan, these fiery trials are necessary. In Romans 5:3–5, Paul says, "We also glory in our sufferings, because we know that suffering produces perseverance; perseverance, character; and character, hope. And hope does not put us to shame, because God's love has been poured out into our hearts through the Holy Spirit, who has been given to us."

One more word about the purpose of fiery trials. In James 1:2–3, it says, "Consider it pure joy, my brothers and sisters, whenever you face trials of many kinds, because you know that the testing of your faith produces perseverance." Time and time again throughout 1 Peter we are told that trials are coming. Trials are neither strange nor surprising. They are necessary in God's plan, serving as his refining judgment and discipline. If you're in the midst of one right now, don't be surprised, and don't let it catch you unknowingly.

This is a broken, fallen world, and God is good. God is faithful when we lose our equilibrium in life, as we're surprised and knocked off course by painful things. We each may have a bit of the prosperity gospel in our system needing to be purged.

The book of 1 Peter ends with these words: "This is the true grace of God. Stand firm in it!" (1 Pet. 5:12, NASB). Peter is helping us stand in the truth of God's amazing grace and lasting hope. He doesn't shy away from saying it will be hard. Life is hard; it can be brutal. God is good. Glory is coming, so stand firm in Christ.

2. Rejoice

The urging to rejoice sounds counterintuitive, even crazy, to many people. Verse thirteen says, "Rejoice inasmuch as you participate in the sufferings of Christ, so that you may be overjoyed when his glory is revealed."

Now that's a mysterious and mystical idea. Somehow, we participate in the sufferings of Jesus so that we may be overjoyed—not just a little joy, but *overjoyed*, running over with joy. Jesus spoke of this often. He lived it out. Luke said it in Luke 6:22–23. The author of Hebrews said it in Hebrews 12:2. James said it in James 1:2. It was pervasive in the early church as a teaching:

> *The Christ-exalting response to suffering is joy.*

Nothing reveals the goodness and the realness of God like someone living through a trial and rejoicing throughout. In Matthew 5:11–12, Jesus says, "Blessed are you when people insult you, persecute you and falsely say all kinds of evil against you because of me. Rejoice and be glad, because great is your reward in heaven." Luke in Acts 5:41 writes, "Then they left the presence of the council, rejoicing that they were counted worthy to suffer dishonor for the name." I'll re-emphasize what Paul says in Romans 5:3–4: "We rejoice in our sufferings, knowing that suffering produces endurance, and endurance produces character, and character produces hope" (ESV).

When a teaching is this clear in the Bible and repeated so often, we should pay attention. We have good reason to rejoice when we understand that pain is for our ultimate good and transformation—and that God is not out to destroy us but to redeem us.

Does it mean we ignore reality, putting our head in the sand and whistling a happy tune amid great pain? The text is not saying you should use your religion as a numbing agent against pain. Don't lean on the promises of God or Christian cliches to get you through life. That's not what this teaching means.

Another passage in 2 Corinthians 6 says we are "sorrowful, yet always rejoicing." We have deep sorrows. Who doesn't have deep sorrows? If you live on earth, and there's a heart beating in your chest, and you've seen even a trace of how dark, evil, and disappointing this world is, then you carry sorrow. Yet we are rejoicing. The longer we trust and follow Jesus, the more our capacity for sorrow will deepen.

> *Our joy will be enhanced, and our hearts will grow.*

We carry sorrows. We face reality, yet God has made us happy in him—because he's good. We're blessed, we've been forgiven, and there's abundant grace at work in our lives. How could we not be joyful? It's not an either-or, sorrow or joy. We hold both.

Dallas Willard said that we experience pain whenever we bump into reality.[11] What kinds of reality have you bumped into lately? When harsh realities come upon you and you bump into them, you *can* have joy—not because the realities are easy but because of Christ. The reality may feel like fire. It hurts; it stings; it burns sometimes. Your joy doesn't come from the trial itself but from the God who is walking with you and transforming you, even in the trial.

C. S. Lewis said, "If you look for truth, you may find comfort in the end: if you look for comfort you will not get either comfort or truth—only soft soap and wishful thinking to begin with and, in the end, despair."[12] We don't find joy by ignoring reality and seeking comfort at all costs. We look beyond the hard realities we face, and we fix our hearts on deeper realities, on the things of God, the things Peter has been pointing us to all throughout his letter.

3. Don't Be Ashamed

How do you respond when the fires come? Don't be ashamed: "If you suffer as a Christian, do not be ashamed" (1 Pet. 4:16). The human ego hates to be shamed, exposed, or crossed. Little embarrassments are horrible, and well, we just don't like to be embarrassed. Christianity, though, is built on a once-shamed Messiah. In 1 Peter 2:4, Peter describes our life in Christ as coming to him, a "living stone rejected by men but in the sight of God chosen and precious" (ESV). We have come to a rejected Christ—thrown out, despised, hated, slandered, spit on, mocked, stripped, and nailed to a tree.

Christ is our forerunner, our sin remover, our hope provider. Christ is our life: "To this you were called, because Christ suffered for you, leaving you an example, so that you should follow in his steps" (1 Pet. 2:21). Objectively speaking, as he was shamed, so we will be shamed.

But Jesus looked to the glory of anticipated joy. He saw joy on the horizon, and he entrusted his soul to a faithful Creator. He looked shame full on and knew it would not have the last word in his story. Shame never stopped him from joyfully trusting in his Father.

That is one of the many things encouraging us to deify and admire Jesus. If Jesus is not your hero yet, let this concept push you over the edge. Jesus walked through tremendous adversity and shame, and he stayed faithful. This same faithfulness is what Peter calls us to. No shame in Christ. None. Be free. Be unashamed of sarcasm, ridicule, abandonment, and suffering. He remains faithful to us and beckons us to faithfulness in him.

4. Praise God

When the fires come, praise God: "If you suffer as a Christian, do not be ashamed, but praise God that you bear that name" (1 Pet. 4:16). In so doing, you show others how your treasure is not in this world but in God.

I bet you've been witness to this as well as experienced it for yourself. When you see godly people walking through fiery ordeals, if you look closely, you will often witness the goodness and the glory of God. Perhaps, by God's mercy, 1 Peter 2:12 may become a reality for us. It says, "So that when they speak against you as evildoers, they may see your good deeds and glorify God." It's an echo of Jesus' Sermon on the Mount in Matthew 5: Be salt and light "that they may see your good deeds and glorify your Father in heaven" (Matt. 5:16).

So whatever form the fiery trial takes, God calls us to not be surprised as though something strange were happening. We should not be ashamed but instead rejoice with souls entrusted to him.

> *Our real treasure is Jesus and not anything this world offers.*

5. Do Good to Others

When the fire comes, do good to others: "Those who suffer according to God's will should commit themselves to their faithful Creator and continue to do good" (1 Pet. 4:19).

It's so tempting to turn inward and let trials consume us. In our self-preoccupation, which often descends into self-pity, we can't see anything but the pain, the trial, the ridicule, the fear, the uncertainty, and the shame.

God allows the broken pieces to display his light.

But when we come out of ourselves and begin to see others, we will realize that the trial and the pain was never about us. It was always about God refining and transforming us. It was about God allowing the broken pieces, the cracks in our lives, to display his light. It was about God leveraging our pain to bring others hope.

Blessing other people when you're in a fire won't take you out of the fire, but it will make you more resilient as you walk through it. In thinking about how Jesus exemplified this, I reread the last few chapters of each Gospel and counted all the good things he did while suffering. Can you imagine knowing you were going to be flogged with leather and glass shards and bones before being beaten and hung on a tree?

Jesus was already suffering at the Passover table, knowing his Father's will. What is the first thing he did? He washed his disciples' feet. He was fully present with them. He thought about them and cared for them, knowing time was running out and he would soon suffer. Yet he washed their feet. Then, when Judas showed up in the garden and led the rabble of Romans to arrest Jesus, Jesus didn't condemn him. He didn't curse him. He stood there, willingly. That's a remarkable thing.

Then when he was being nailed to the cross, he prayed for the soldiers, *Father, forgive them*, begging his Father to forgive them for murdering the Son of God. And before he took his last breath, he looked down from the cross and saw his mom, one more piece of unfinished business he had to take care of. He looked over at his best friend, John, and asked him to take care of his mother. John agreed.

The last good thing he did—this is the one that really gets me—was for a man hanging next to him, dying because he had done a bad thing. The other two men Jesus was crucified with were guilty. They were receiving the justice of the state. Jesus was not. He was perfect and innocent. Instead of writhing in self-pity, he listened to the man's request: "Jesus, remember me when you come into your kingdom" (Luke 23:42).

I don't know where that man's faith came from. We don't know anything more of his story. All we know is that without hesitation, without preaching to him or asking questions, Jesus responded, "Truly I tell you, today you will be with me in paradise" (Luke 23:43).

In your suffering, God has a plan. Trust the Lord. "Blessed is the one who perseveres under trial because, having stood the test, that person will receive the crown of life that the Lord has promised to those who love him" (James 1:12). There is a spectacular reward for those who stay the course. Don't numb the pain, but instead "let perseverance finish its work so that you may be mature and complete, not lacking anything" (James 1:4).

You're amazing, Jesus. We thank you for simply being who you are and for leaving us an example that we may follow in your steps. Remind us yet again—because we tend to forget—that you can feed our souls in ways bread never could. Jesus, from the bottom of our hearts, with everything in us, we thank you for pouring out your blood. Your blood was spilled, and it was all for us. You served others, even as terrible things happened to you. We're in awe. Help us to open our hearts to receive your grace and forgiveness again.

We ask you with hungry and desperate hearts to come and teach us again. Where there is death, bring life. Where there is confusion, bring clarity. Where there is discouragement, bring hope. Where there is pride, give us humility. Where there is division, bring unity. Where there is depletion, give us fullness.

Jesus, help us to be like you. When life turns up the heat and the fires rage, help us not to turn inward, but to serve others. Help your disciples to look to each other before looking to ourselves; help us to serve others with joy and self-sacrificing love. We celebrate your faithfulness. When we are faithless, you are faithful. Without you, there would be no living hope. With you, we can be the most hopeful people on the planet, and we give you praise. In Jesus name, amen.

Lessons for Elders— and for Us All

A Sermon on 1 Peter 5:1–6

To the elders among you, I appeal as a fellow elder and a witness of Christ's sufferings who also will share in the glory to be revealed: Be shepherds of God's flock that is under your care, watching over them—not because you must, but because you are willing, as God wants you to be; not pursuing dishonest gain, but eager to serve; not lording it over those entrusted to you, but being examples to the flock. And when the Chief Shepherd appears, you will receive the crown of glory that will never fade away. In the same way, you who are younger, submit yourselves to your elders. All of you, clothe yourselves with humility toward one another, because: "God opposes the proud but shows favor to the humble." Humble yourselves, therefore, under God's mighty hand, that he may lift you up in due time.

— 1 Pet. 5:1–6

Peter weaves the theme of living hope through chapters one and two, and then in chapter three he starts to talk about suffering. Peter says that suffering well reveals the goodness and glory of God like nothing else can. You have been given living hope. Relying on any other form of hope is no hope at all. Any other hope is a dead hope. There is no hope apart from the empty tomb of Jesus.

> There is no hope apart from the empty tomb of Jesus.

In chapter five, Peter takes yet another unexpected turn. Why is he addressing elders?

Turning to Elders

In the New International Version of the Bible, a word is omitted that can be found in the New American Standard Bible: "*Therefore*, I urge elders among you, as your fellow elder and a witness of the sufferings of Christ, and one who is also a fellow partaker of the glory that is to be revealed" (1 Pet. 5:1). The first word of verse one is an important word because it means "in view of everything I've said, I'm going to talk to the elders now." There is a very intentional purpose for what Peter is doing.

I need to point out how the text assumes the church is being led by a group of elders. In the first century, churches weren't led by a single person but by a plurality of God-ordained, spiritually mature, proven-over-time men who collectively shepherded God's flock. They weren't leading from a place driven by bottom lines and budgets and competition with the others in town. They were shepherds caring for the church, discerning the will of God together in community. Have we not seen overwhelming reasons why the pastor-king, one-man-show church model doesn't work? It's not healthy. It's not biblical.

This is not to throw stones, but Scripture couldn't be any clearer. The church is not a corporation. It's a different kingdom, with a different king and very different definitions of success, beauty, goodness, humility, submission, love, truth, and sacrifice.

Okay, back to the question. Why does Peter address the elders?

The Fiery Ordeal

Peter has warned the church about a fiery ordeal. He says in verse thirteen of chapter four that followers of Jesus may share in the sufferings of Christ for a season and then exalt in the glory of Christ when he comes. In chapter four, verse seventeen, he explains why the fiery trial is coming on the church: "For it is time for judgment to begin with the household of God; and if it begins with us first, what will be the outcome for those who do not obey the gospel of God?" (1 Peter 4:17, NASB). This means that—for the whole church, not just for the elders—the fiery ordeal that comes as a punishment, as a condemnation, on unbelievers hits the church first as a fire of purification and refining.

Two background texts in the Old Testament help make sense of the principle Peter is communicating. The first one is Ezekiel 9. This is one of the passages in the Old Testament that you read and think, *Whoa, the wrath of God is on full display.* It comes first to his own people and then moves to the surrounding culture.

If Peter has in mind the way God once began judgment in his own house, he may be saying, *I know it's getting hard in Rome and in the provinces and cities, but it's going to start here in the church. In the church, it will start with the elders, those who lead.* Maybe he's trying to exhort and encourage those elders to press on during severe testing.

The second background text is Malachi 3, where God says his messenger will come to his temple. In the same way Peter speaks of in 1 Peter 2:5, Malachi 3 speaks of an encounter God will have not with the world but with his own people: "Who can endure the day of his coming? Who can stand when he appears? For he will be like a refiner's fire. . . . He will sit as a refiner and purifier of silver; he will purify the Levites and refine them like gold and silver" (Mal. 3:2–3). The Levites are priests, the equivalent in the Old Testament of our elders.

Now it's true that 1 Peter 2 says all believers are priests, but it's not easy for a leader to read this and fail to see that the refining fire of God's judgment comes to the leadership first. It's a wonderful and sobering thing to be an elder in the church that Jesus purchased with his own blood. This is worth noting: If the elders lead the church into strength and vitality and fruitfulness and unity as they're charged to do, they will also lead the church into the refiner's fire of God's purifying judgment. They will not stand above the church or outside the church, giving suggestions on how we should cope with the fires of life. They will lead the church into the fire. They will go first; they will feel the heat first, and it will be hottest for them.

So when Peter says in verse one that he's "a fellow elder," he's not saying, "I have a special title." He could have called himself an apostle, and that would have been true. He's saying, "I'm with you, elders. I know it's hard. I know the fires are raging, but I am with you. I stand with you in that place of desperation. I've seen and experienced the suffering of Jesus in my own life. I stand with you in utter dependency on God as the trials of life turn up their heat and test us all."

Peter is trying to pump some hope into those elders. Peter believes that those elders need a special message at the end of his letter. Fire is painful, judgment is serious, and the stakes for the church are high. Peter has three words of wisdom for elders in this text—wisdom that also applies to anyone who seeks to make disciples of Jesus. It's especially meant for elders, but there's something for all of us in his words.

1. Go All In

The first pearl of wisdom is to go all in. Don't hold back.

> Be shepherds of God's flock that is under your care, watching over them—not because you must, but because you are willing. (1 Pet. 5:2)

Peter warns the elders against drifting into a heartless, distracted, or detached pattern of ministry that requires external motivation or compulsion. Don't be afraid of doing what you're called to do.

Now, it may not have been apathy, but fear that the elders were dealing with. This is why we should never pressure anyone to be an elder. A man needs to feel called and confirmed. Then, once he becomes an elder, he should shepherd the flock willingly and from the heart.

2. Check Your Motives

Peter warns the elders against greed, against the lust for money, power, and prestige. Verse two says to shepherd the flock, "not pursuing dishonest gain, but eager to serve." In other words, don't lead for the wrong reasons.

Have you ever seen a bad elder before? There are elders who want power and influence, and they enter into the elder group for less than honorable reasons. I've seen it. I've been hurt by it. I've sadly watched churches be destroyed by it.

Peter says that rather than being a prideful elder or leader, do your ministry with eagerness, leaning in and loving your work. Find joy in serving the church of Jesus Christ. Hebrews 13 says let the elders minister "with joy and not with grief, for this would be unprofitable for you" (Heb. 13:17, NASB).

3. Lead with Humility

Verse three says to shepherd the flock, "not lording it over those entrusted to you." Notice the phrase "entrusted to you." I immediately thought of my children, who are entrusted to my wife and me for a season until they leave our care. They are ultimately not mine. I don't own them. They belong to God. That's the way Peter talks about the churches. Don't think a church is all yours. These are not *your* people. They are entrusted to you, so treat them accordingly. Be shepherds and examples for them.

He warns the elders to reject pride. Pride is the failure to realize how deeply desperate we are for Jesus. It's refusing to grasp that, without Jesus, we can do nothing. The proud heart feels like it can be self-reliant, and self-reliance becomes blinding arrogance.

Lead like Jesus—with humility. When that fiery ordeal comes to you first, lead by example. Don't bail on the process; don't escape it; don't run from it; but walk through it alongside the sheep.

A Shared Mission

Peter ends with one final word of hope. Of course he would. Peter saw Jesus rise from the dead. How could he not brim over with hope in every verse?

> When the Chief Shepherd appears, you will receive the crown of glory that will never fade away. (1 Pet. 5:4)

There may be times when the elders feel that the refining fire is too hot. It can be tempting to think that if it takes so much fire to burn away our sin, laziness, greed, pride, and idolatry, then maybe it's not worth it. If it takes so much pain, maybe we should give up. To those who feel tempted to walk away, Peter says there will be a day when the Chief Shepherd, the lead elder, will appear, and it will be so satisfying that all the serving, all the tears, all the late-night prayers, all the agony, and all the work will be worth it. There will be a day for all of us when we stand before him, and it will be really, really, really good.

Peter ends the passage with a brief word to those who are younger. I'll let you decide if you fit that description. "Submit yourself to your elders" (1 Pet. 5:5); that's what it says.

I would encourage all of us—I put myself in the boat right there with you—to ask ourselves, *What do our elders call us to do as a church?* If you're a member at a church, you have a membership covenant. This is not like joining Costco. It's a little different than that. We're in this together. Together, we share a mission. We need each other, and we are embarking on a journey that requires supernatural help. It's a big deal.

> We should give our elders the respect, the honor, and the trust they are due.

Cultivating Humility

The key principle for the whole passage begins in verse five and continues to the end of the passage: "All of you"—elders, young people, everyone—"clothe yourselves with humility toward one another, because, 'God opposes the proud but shows favor to the humble'" (1 Pet. 5:5).

We all know what humility is and what it isn't. You know it when you see it. We're naturally drawn to it because it's attractive and refreshing. Who doesn't want to be around a humble, life-giving person? We also feel repelled by humility's opposite. Everyone loves humility, and we're drawn to humble people. But in my experience, hardly anyone wants to put in the necessary work to cultivate humility.

We're not born humble. Humility is not the default setting of the human heart. Selfishness is, and the only way to break free from it is to partner with the Holy Spirit in cultivating humility over time. God brings us humility in two ways: through spiritual disciplines and through suffering. We are broken by the trials of life and by spiritual disciplines—which disciples of Jesus have been practicing for hundreds of years. Six things are required if you want to be a humble person.

1. *Live in the presence of God.* Practice the presence of God. Don't forget about him. Live moment by moment in his presence because it's impossible to be prideful and aware of God's presence at the same time. There's only one God, right?

2. *Confess sin.* I don't mean in your prayer closet. Confess your sin to another person. Not because that's the only way you can receive forgiveness or because you're under obligation to do so, but because you want to be free from the prison of sin and you want to cultivate the fruit of humility. Speaking the truths that you did wrong, you need help, and you need to repent has a way of pouring humility into a heart.

3. *Connect deeply with disciples.* This means transparent relationships with other disciples, not flying solo as a spiritual Christian who doesn't really have time to befriend others and walk in the light.

4. *Serve other people who can't repay you.* Ask God to open doors for you to really serve—not for what you can get, but for what you can give.

5. *Befriend people who won't enhance your status.* Every disciple of Jesus should have a few friends who don't quite make sense from the world's perspective. Friendship in our day is often transactional, selfish, and shallow. The church should completely reject that way of relationships. We should have open, hospitable hearts, and we should befriend people not because of what they have to offer. Jesus descended from heaven to earth and befriended us.

6. *Abide in Christ.* Connecting with Jesus is life-changing. A meaningful and intimate walk with Christ gives more perspective, more peace, and more passion for his kingdom than we could imagine. If you haven't read John 15 in a while, I encourage you to pour deeply over those words.

Make humility a top priority in your life.

So what's your plan to grow in humility? Without a plan, there won't be fruit. If you intend on being a life-giving person who loves well and who is faithful to what the Bible calls you to do, make humility a top priority in your life. Do anything and everything you can to cultivate it as a fruit. Others will be blessed when you grow in humility.

Lord, I ask you to help me be humble. Would you lessen our pride? Would you forgive us for our arrogance and how our self-centeredness has hurt others? Help us to find tangible strategies and disciplines to help us grow in humility. We pray for our elders: Lord Jesus, would you bless, encourage, empower, protect, and personally attend to each elder of your church? Give them joy, give them strength, and give them wisdom. Would you enrich their marriages and touch their families, their children, and their grandchildren? Would you bless their health? Would you give them a sense of your nearness? Would you grant them continued unity, protect them from division and distraction, and make them one? And would you help us to be members of the body of Christ who serves, loves, prays, and disciples with a surrendered, joyful spirit? Jesus, this is your church. You alone get to determine who we are and where we are going. We lift you up as the head of the body. Help us to receive your authority as a gift of grace, not a threat. Jesus, we offer ourselves to you now. Every part of our lives—sin, shame, fears, stress, and pride—we give it all to you. I pray in your name, amen.

Final Exhortations

A Sermon on 1 Peter 5:7–9

> *Cast all your anxiety on him because he cares for you. Be alert and of sober mind. Your enemy the devil prowls around like a roaring lion looking for someone to devour. Resist him, standing firm in the faith, because you know that the family of believers throughout the world is undergoing the same kind of sufferings.*
>
> *— 1 Pet. 5:7–9*

n Oklahoma City, Oklahoma, they have a sacred symbol, a sprawl-
ing, shade-bearing, eighty-year-old American Elm. Tourists drive for
miles to see this tree; they pose for pictures and would protect it at all
costs. The tree adorns posters and letterheads. Other trees grow larger,
fuller, even greener, but none is as cherished as this tree.

The city treasures the tree not because of what it looks like but
because of its endurance. You see, the tree survived the Oklahoma
City bombing. Timothy McVeigh parked his death-laden truck only
yards away from this tree. His malice killed 168 people, wounded
over six hundred more, destroyed the Alfred P. Murrah Federal Building, and buried the tree in rubble.

No one expected the tree to survive. No one gave the tree hope.
But then it began to bud sprouts, new life pressing through the marred
surface. Green leaves pushed away the soot, and life resurrected from
an acre of death. People felt that the tree modeled the resilience the
victims desired, so they gave the elm a name: the Survivor Tree.

Followers of Jesus are very much like that tree. During the trials
of life, we grow, and we bear fruit—because we're rooted in the giver
of life. We rely on Jesus day by day, and he fills us with living hope.
Peter presents three exhortations in this passage to help us bear fruit
in trials.

1. Let Go

Verse seven says, "Cast all your anxiety on him." Cast away your burdens; don't hold on to them. I wonder what all prevents us from doing
that. The command to offload your worries, fears, and anxieties—to
let God be God and know that you are not—appears in every section
of the Bible.

Anxiety is all the rage these days. We're all overwhelmed. Anxiety
is the word of our day. We're up at night with worry or stress. We're
over-engaged, overworked, and overstimulated. Some wear stress and
chaos like a badge of honor, like somehow the more overwhelmed you
are, the more important you are and the more significant your life is,

the more impressive you are in the race of life. Every bit of it goes back to pride. Humanity is self-deluded in thinking everything relies and depends upon us.

No one is strong enough. No one is wise enough. No one is healthy enough. No one is spiritual enough or righteous enough or good enough to handle life on their own. You can't hold on to worry and have peace at the same time. But when we let God have our worries, we receive peace that surpasses our understanding—otherworldly, transcendent peace that only comes from the God of peace.

Why don't we exchange stress and worry for peace? Why don't we take hold of what Jesus has already made available to us? His peace is not the absence of conflict. It's not the absence of pain. It's not the absence of struggle. His peace is the presence of God guiding us. God cares for us. Because of that we can let go. We can let go with a peaceful and joyful conscience. His care is not a cliche, and it's not wishful thinking; it's the truth.

God sees your life. He hears your prayers.

As believers in the God whom Jesus came to perfectly reveal, we don't have to wonder if he cares. We know he does. The God of the universe, our Creator, is intimately aware of and deeply involved in what we're walking through.

Jesus said, "I am the Good Shepherd" (John 10:11). If you want to see what God is like, look at a shepherd tending sheep. It's personal. It's a warm, attentive, engaged glimpse of God watching over us, protecting us, leading us, guiding us, correcting us, transforming us, and redeeming our stories. This truth about how God cares for you should enable you to walk through life not worrying over every bump in the road, but letting go and trusting in the God of living hope.

2. Wake Up

First Peter 5:8 says, "Be alert and of sober mind." Live with a posture of spiritual wakefulness; be vigilant about your life. Do you live as though you know what's at stake?

Life and death hang in the balance—not only yours but those around you. We live in a broken, twisted, fallen world. You've been called to live in the light and be a herald of hope. Your life affects others. It's far from unimportant.

Peter uses intense, graphic language to help us understand this. Verse eight says, "Your enemy the devil prowls around like a roaring lion looking for someone to devour." Have you ever seen a lion prowl or roar? Lions have teeth—big, sharp, destructive teeth. They have claws. They stalk their prey, and when they see their prey become weak and vulnerable, they pounce. The devil does the same, and he does it well.

Jack Handey is known for his odd sense of humor frequently expressed in the old *Saturday Night Live* segment called "Deep Thoughts by Jack Handey." He wrote a weird, obscure book called *Fuzzy Memories*.[13] In it, he relates the story of a bully from his childhood who daily demanded his lunch money. Because Handey was smaller than the bully, he gave his money away. Five dollars was a lot of money though, so he wanted to fight back. Jack thought he'd start taking karate lessons. The only problem was that the karate instructor wanted ten dollars per lesson. Jack realized he could either pay the bully five dollars or the karate instructor ten—not a difficult decision. So he gave up the idea of karate, thinking, *It's cheaper to just pay the bully.*

Unfortunately, many of us believers have the same attitude about the devil and his temptations. He whispers lies into our hearts, yet we act like it's easier to pay the bully than learn how to fight. How is this lion coming for you? Where are you weak? What lies are you most tempted to believe? He uses two weapons against all of God's children: temptation and suffering. The two come in tandem.

Here's how it often works: Suffering blinds us to the goodness of God. It induces spiritual fatigue. Then the temptations come—to numb pain, to escape from reality. We are tempted to assume the role of God, tempted to try and produce outcomes only God is powerful enough to produce. The devil's goal is to destroy your confidence in God and convince you faith is a lie. Because of this, it's so important to cultivate spiritual wakefulness. We need be awake to what's happening in us and around us.

3. Stand Firm

Stay the course.

Verse nine says, "Resist him, standing firm in the faith." We engage the devil in battle by standing firm in the faith. The faith Peter refers to isn't in the prevailing myths of our culture or in our emotions. Myths and feelings fade. They mislead. Our calling is to stand firm with a living hope in a living faith.

A former Muslim named Abdu Murray wrote a book called *Saving Truth*.[14] He talks in the book about the dominant worldviews our culture has embraced in the last several years. He talks about postmodernism first. The claim of postmodernism is that there is no objective truth; it's all relative. You have an understanding of reality, and that's fantastic for you, but don't foist that on others. If you force someone else to embrace your truth, that's an act of aggression. The goal of postmodernism is to eradicate any idea of objective truth. But we all know that worldview is not workable. It's not real. It's just unlivable. We don't truly believe that truth is relative. We know that some things are true and some things are not.

That worldview is going out of style, and Murray says what's replaced it is something even more sinister. He calls it "post-truth." Postmodernism has given way to post-truth. It elevates feelings and preferences over facts and truth. The proponents of the post-truth mentality don't deny that truth exists, but they value feelings or preferences above it. It goes something like this: *There is objective truth. But if it doesn't match up with my opinions, preferences, feelings, or views, I don't care.*

There is a widespread ignorance, removal, and devaluation of truth, both with postmodernism and the emerging post-truth perspective. The only way we can resist the devil with his deceptions and vicious tactics of warfare against us is to stand firm in the faith.

> *Stand firm.*

Not in our culture and certainly not in emotion, but in the faith that Jesus has given you. How can you do that? You can because you're not alone. First Peter 5:9 says, to paraphrase, *You know that the family of believers throughout the world is undergoing the same kind of sufferings.* Faith, hope, joy, and love wither away and die in isolation. The current culture cultivates isolation, which makes the church even more critical. May we be a church where no one stands alone, where everyone can know they are engulfed in the love of God, where there rests no doubt in whether God is with them or for them, and where they know they have a community.

May we be a church where no one stands alone.

One Final Word of Hope

Thinking about God and the way he works in the world, it's tempting to believe God will somehow create for us a life of no pain, no loss, no heartache, and no fear—if we only do all the right things, avoid sin, and perform well. Peter doesn't stand for believing such destructive myths. He says suffering is real and normal. When the realities of this dark, evil, rapidly decaying world find themselves in your life, hold on to your living hope.

We believe—and stand firm in the faith—that the same Jesus who came as a baby will return as a conquering King, and the same Jesus who walked out of his own grave will raise us from our graves. All sadness will be undone, and every sign of death will be erased forever. The clock is ticking on injustice, hatred, division, and evil.

Those of us who have been born again into a living hope by the resurrection of Jesus Christ from the dead can hear that clock ticking. We know it's only a matter of time until our enemy, the devil, will be finally and fully put in his place. Though we can't experience it fully, we can go ahead and live in victory, not because of what we've done but because of what our King, our risen Lord Jesus, has done.

Peter's final word of hope: "The God of all grace, who called you to his eternal glory in Christ, after you've suffered a little while, will himself restore you and make you strong, firm and steadfast" (1 Pet. 5:10). I love the way he uses "a little while." The thing about suffering is that it feels like forever. But Peter says it's only for a little while. Hang in there. God himself will restore you. In 2 Corinthians 4:18, Paul says, "We fix our eyes not on what is seen, but on what is unseen, because what is seen is temporary, but what is unseen is eternal."

In the name of Jesus, I say to those of you who are anxious and fearful and worried: You are seen. Your prayers are heard. Your entire life is being carefully watched over by God. Cast your cares on him. He can handle it. Let your burdens go, and let God be God.

In the name of Jesus, I say to those of you who are coasting through life unaware that you're being attacked: Wake up. The devil hates you. He hates your family, your marriage, and your church, and he hates Jesus more than anybody else. Resist him, take up the armor of God, and fight.

In the name of Jesus, I say to you: We are not our struggles. We all need help. We all face trials and temptations. Let us move toward each other and lock arms as the storms of life rage and thunder against us. Let us stand firm together and trust that he will restore us—maybe not in this life, but in the resurrected life to come.

To him be the power and glory forever and ever.

Jesus, we long to hear your voice. We're desperate for your wisdom, so we open our lives and hearts up to you. We pray in your name, amen.

Notes

1. Thesaurus.com, s.v. "hope (*n.*)," thesaurus.com/browse/hope.

2. Dana Sparks, "In the Loop: Lung Transplant Recipient's First Breath Goes Viral," *Mayo Clinic News Network*, March 6, 2018, newsnetwork.mayoclinic.org/discussion/in-the-loop-lung-transplant-recipients-first-breath-goes-viral; see also inspiremore.com/transplant-patient-breathes and cff.org/community-posts/2018-03/time-we-went-viral-and-where-we-actually-are-today.

3. Elaine Lipworth, "'My Best Character Trait? I'm a Pretty Good Lover. My Worst? Not Being Better': Inside the Head of . . . Jeff Bridges," *DailyMail.com*, September 14, 2013, dailymail.co.uk/home/event/article-2418985/Jeff-Bridges-My-best-character-trait-Im-pretty-good-lover-My-worst-Not-better.html.

4. David Kinnaman and Gabe Lyons, *UnChristian: What a New Generation Really Thinks About Christianity . . . and Why It Matters* (Grand Rapids, Michigan: Baker Books, 2007), 42.

5. Dave Ramsey, "No Gossip Policy," *EntreLeadership*, May 9, 2018, video, 2:52, youtube.com/watch?v=EFpANOYMkjk.

6. Frederica Mathewes-Green, *The Jesus Prayer: The Ancient Desert Prayer That Tunes the Heart to God* (Brewster, MA: Paraclete Press, 2009), xiv.

7. Austin Farrer, *The Truth-Seeking Heart: Austin Farrer and His Writings*, ed. Ann Loades and Robert MacSwain (London: Canterbury Press Norwich, 2006), 131.

8. Lucian, *The Passing of Peregrinus*, 11–13.

9. Edmund P. Clowney, "The Biblical Theology of the Church," *RPM*, 17.1 (December 28, 2014 to January 3, 2015), thirdmill.org/magazine/article.asp/link/ed_clowney%5Ebt_church.1.html.

10. Tullian Tchividjian, "Our Calling, Our Spheres," *Christianity Today*, Summer 2010, christianitytoday.com/pastors/2010/summer/ourcallingspheres.html.

11. John Ortberg, "Dallas Willard, a Man from Another 'Time Zone,'" *Christianity Today*, May 8, 2013, christianitytoday.com/ct/2013/may-web-only/man-from-another-time-zone.html.

12. C. S. Lewis, *Mere Christianity* (1952; repr., New York: Macmillan, 1986), 25.

13. Jack Handey, *Fuzzy Memories* (Kansas City, MO: Andrews McMeel Publishing, 1996).

14. Abdu Murray, *Saving Truth* (Grand Rapids, Michigan: Zondervan, 2018), 12–15.

Discussion Questions

Matt Patrick

Chapter 1: The Mythical Hope

1. Read 1 Peter 1:3–4 aloud: "Praise be to the God and Father of our Lord Jesus Christ! In his great mercy he has given us new birth into a living hope through the resurrection of Jesus Christ from the dead, and into an inheritance that can never perish, spoil, or fade." What stands out to you from this passage?
2. Jesus is alive. Hope is not a strategy or sentimental feeling; hope is a person. How does the resurrection of Christ animate our hope as his people?
3. What false gods are you tempted to place your hope in? How and why do they fail us?
4. Myth 2 says, "Hope fades over time." How can eternal hope through Christ animate our everyday life?
5. How have you misunderstood hope in the past? What is your living hope like now?

Chapter 2: A Claim, a Command, and a Craving

1. Read 1 Peter 1:23 aloud: "For you have been born again, not of perishable seed, but of imperishable, through the living and enduring word of God." What stands out to you from this passage?
2. How does the apostle Peter ground Christian hope in an inheritance that can never perish?

3. What does Peter mean by referring to every Christ follower as someone who has been "born again"?
4. What is God's overall goal for us when we experience trials and seasons of suffering? How does suffering invite us to experience God's heart?
5. How does having living hope change everything? How can you live your everyday life differently because of having a living hope versus a dead one?

Chapter 3: Remember Who You Are

1. Read 1 Peter 2:5 aloud: "You also, like living stones, are being built into a spiritual house to be a holy priesthood." What stands out to you from this passage?
2. How does God's "gracious posture" enable us to obey him in our everyday lives?
3. How does being God's "prized possession" free us from trying to prove ourselves to others?
4. How is God calling you to embody his character in your vocation, to participate in the royal priesthood of God's people through your work?
5. How does having living hope change your view of yourself? How can you build up others to see who they are in Christ too?

Chapter 4: Become Who You Are

1. Read 1 Peter 2:16 aloud: "Live as free people, but do not use your freedom as a cover-up for evil; live as God's slaves." What stands out to you from this passage?
2. Josh said, "Only when we reach the end of our resources can he use us mightily." How was this true for Peter's life?
3. How do God's people live differently as "exiles" in a foreign and fallen world?
4. Where is God calling you to abstain in order to grow more fully into your identity in Christ?

5. How does having living hope moves us closer to Christ? How is your life different now that you have living hope than it was when you had a dead one?

Chapter 5: Ruthless Trust

1. Read 1 Peter 2:21 aloud: "To this you were called, because Christ suffered for you, leaving you an example, that you should follow in his steps." What stands out to you from this passage?
2. In Christ, we have an inheritance that is eternal, being "kept in heaven." How does that free you as you live in an unpredictable, fleeting, and fallen world?
3. Why is hope for Christians oriented toward the future?
4. How does our suffering follow the example of Christ's suffering?
5. How does having living hope affect your faith and trust in God? How can you live out ruthless trust?

Chapter 6: A Sacred Covenant

1. Read 1 Peter 3:1, 7 aloud: "Wives, in the same way submit yourselves to your own husbands . . . . Husbands, in the same way be considerate as you live with your wives." What stands out to you from this passage?
2. On the journey of following Jesus, how is the notion of "submission" a freeing rather than a binding action? Unpack how the practice of submission characterizes all relationships in the kingdom of God.
3. Josh said, "Submission is the hallmark of every great marriage." How so?
4. How does the covenant between husband and wife mirror God's covenant with his people?
5. How does having living hope affect your view of submission? In what ways has your heart been softened toward submission?

Chapter 7: Strengthened for Suffering

1. Read 1 Peter 3:15 aloud: "But in your hearts revere Christ as Lord. Always be prepared to give an answer to everyone who asks you to give the reason for the hope that you have." What stands out to you from this passage?
2. Hope in God's people isn't shaken by every cultural twist or turn or fueled by worldly fears. How is the living hope of Jesus countercultural in our world?
3. Josh said, "Our hope is fixed on a person who has overcome death." How might resurrection hope anchor your soul while enduring suffering and trials?
4. Josh said, "Nothing reveals the glory and reality of God like a believer who suffers. We live in a culture of pain avoidance. We will do anything and everything we can to avoid pain— shortcuts, eject buttons, numbing agents, anything to opt out of pain." Unpack this and apply it to your own life.
5. Josh said, "My distractions aren't working." How might admitting our empty distractions and numbing agents free us to embrace the living, unshakeable hope of the risen Christ?
6. How does having living hope change the way you view suffering? How has your perspective been broadened when it comes to sorrow and suffering?

Chapter 8: Walking Through the Fire

1. Read 1 Peter 4:13 aloud: "But rejoice inasmuch as you participate in the sufferings of Christ, so that you may be overjoyed when his glory is revealed." What stands out to you from this passage?
2. We shouldn't be surprised by trials. This should free us from unnecessary disappointment. How might that help and enable Christians to suffer well?
3. Joy and sorrow, hope and pain: How do these tensions characterize seasons of suffering for followers of Jesus?

4. Unpack how Jesus himself held these in tension during his own suffering?

5. How does having living hope change the way you approach trials or seasons of sorrow? What can you do differently in moments of trial or heartache?

Chapter 9: Lessons for Elders—and for Us All

1. Read 1 Peter 5:5 aloud: "All of you, clothe yourselves with humility toward one another, because: God opposes the proud but shows favor to the humble." What stands out to you from this passage?

2. How does humility play a crucial role in the church? That is, how does trusting in God's faithfulness through pain help God's church?

3. How is humility attractive and how is pride distasteful in the church (especially when seen in elders or church leaders)?

4. Humility takes practice. Talk through the six action items listed to cultivate humility in your own life: *Live in the presence of God. Confess sin. Connect deeply with disciples. Serve other people who can't repay you. Befriend people who won't enhance your status. Abide in Christ.*

5. How does having living hope change the way you treat people? What can you do differently in your relationships to reflect the humility of Christ?

Chapter 10: Final Exhortations

1. Read 1 Peter 5:9 aloud: "Resist him, standing firm in the faith, because you know that the family of believers throughout the world is undergoing the same kind of sufferings." What stands out to you from this passage?

2. "Cast all your anxiety on him," Peter says in 1 Peter 5:7. That's an incredibly freeing exhortation. Do you believe Jesus can handle *all* your anxiety or worry?

3. In a culture of hurry and worry, busyness and stress, how do you long for Jesus to "lighten" the burden of living in a fallen world?
4. What has been your greatest takeaway from this book?
5. How does having living hope change the way you think and live? What specifically will you do differently in your life where suffering and hope are concerned?

About the Author

JOSH PATRICK has lived in heaven since January 2019. He was a well-loved preacher and author, and everyone thought of him as their best friend. His main desire was to share the hope of Christ with anyone willing to listen. He worked at several churches over the years, with his last home congregation being Harpeth Christian Church in Franklin, Tennessee. His three daughters, Lilly, Joy, and Sarah, along with his wife, Joni, strive to carry out his legacy every single day.

Photo of Josh Patrick at Harpeth Christian Church during the "Living Hope" sermon series featured in this book.